gage

Cornerstones

CANADIAN LANGUAGE ARTS

Anthology 4b

gage EDUCATIONAL PUBLISHING COMPANY
A DIVISION OF CANADA PUBLISHING CORPORATION
Vancouver · Calgary · Toronto · London · Halifax

Canadian Cataloguing in Publication Data

McClymont, Christine
Cornerstones: Canadian language arts 4b

ISBN 0-7715-1201-5

1. Readers (Elementary).   I. Lashmar, patrick.   II. Titl

PE1121.M327 1998   428.6   C97-932213-8

Researchers: Todd Mercer, Monika Croydon

Cover Illustration: Philippe Béha

Acknowledgments

Every reasonable effort has been made to trace ownership of copyrighted material. Information that would enable the publisher to correct any reference or credit in future editions would be appreciated.

7 "Oh, Joyous House" by Richard Janzen from *Miracles: Poems by Children of the English-Speaking World* edited by Richard Lewis (Simon & Schuster, 1966). ©1966 by Richard Lewis. Distributed by The Touchstone Center for Children, Inc., New York, NY. / 8 From *Roses Sing on New Snow*. Text ©1991 by Paul Yee. Illustrations ©1991 by Harvey Chan. A Groundwood Book/Douglas & McIntyre. / 18 Material from *A Pioneer Story* by Barbara Greenwood and Heather Collins. By permission of Kids Can Press, Ltd., Toronto. Text ©1994 by Barbara Greenwood. Illustrations ©1994 by Heather Collins. / 24, 26 "Klaudia" and "Randy and Aaron" excerpted from *The Families Book* by Arlene Erlbach. ©1996 Free Spirit Publishing, Minneapolis, MN. / 25 "Tam" from *Families: A Celebration of Diversity, Commitment, and Love* by Aylette Jenness. ©1990 by Aylette Jenness (Houghton Mifflin Company, 1990). By permission of Aylette Jenness. / 30 "Call It a Miracle" by Anne Carter. ©1998 Anne Carter. / 36 "Mad" by Beth Tossell from *Ten-Second Rain Showers*. ©1996 by Beth Tossell. / 36, 37 "Glad to Be Alive" by Capricia Quick and "Forever and a Day" by Heather Lachman from *Ten-Second Rain Showers* compiled by Sandford Lyne (Simon & Schuster Books for Young Readers ©1996). Reprinted with permission of Sandford Lyne. / 38 *In the Garden* by Carolyn Marie Mamchur with Meguido Zola. By permission of Carolyn Marie Mamchur and Pemmican Publications, Inc. / 46 *You Can Go Home Again* by Jirina Marton. ©1994 by Jirina Marton. By permission of Jirina Marton and Annick Press Ltd. / 58 "Skywriting" from *Sky Words* by Marilyn Singer. Text ©1994 Marilyn Singer. Selected illustrations ©1994 Deborah Kogan. By permission of Atheneum Books for Young Readers. / 60 *Balloon Ride*. ©1991 by Evelyn Clarke Mott. By permission of Walker and Company, New York. / 68 "Get a Rise Out of Air" from *Balloon Science* by Etta Kaner. Text ©1989 by Etta Kaner. By permission of Kids Can Press, Ltd., Toronto. / 72 "The Sun: Earth's Star" from *The Sun* by Paulette Bourgeois and Bill Slavin. Text ©1995 Paulette Bourgeois. Selected illustrations ©1995 by Bill Slavin. By permission of Kid's Can Press, Ltd., Toronto. / 78 *Northern Lights: The Soccer Trails* ©1993 Text ©Michael Arvaarluk Kusugak. Selected illustrations ©Vladyana Krykorka. Published by Annick Press Ltd. / 92 "Starry Summer Night" by Diane Bailey and Drew McKibben. By permission of the authors. / 100 "Dear Earth" by Karla Kuskin. Text ©1993 by Karla Kuskin. By permission of Dutton Children's Books. / 103 "Dragonbrag" from *The Dragons are Singing Tonight* by Jack Prelutsky. Text ©1993 by Jack Prelutsky. By permission of Greenwillow Books. / 104 "Castles and Keeps" by Christopher Maynard from *Incredible Castles and Knights* (Dorling Kindersley Children's Books). / 106 "Growing Up in a Spanish Castle" by Chris and Melanie Rice from *How Children Lived*. ©1995 by Dorling Kindersley Children's Books. / 108 "The Inside Story," originally entitled "Home Life," by Philip Steele from *Castles* © Larousse PLC 1995. By permission of Larousse Kingfisher Chambers, New York. / 112 "The Sword in the Stone" from *The Adventures of King Arthur*. Retold by Angela Wilkes. From *The Adventures of King Arthur*. By permission of Usborne Publishing ©Usborne Publishing Ltd. 1989, 1981. / 120 *Harald and the Giant Knight*.

Text and selected illustrations ©1982 by Donald Carrick. By permission Clarion Books/Houghton Mifflin Company. / 145 From *Poets Go Wishin* selected by Lilian Moore. ©1975 Lilian Moore. By permission of Marian Reiner for the author. / 146 "The Boa," "The Firefly," and "The Anteate from *Beast Feast*, ©1994 by Douglas Florian. By permission of Harcourt Brace & Company. / 147 "Empty circus tent" by George Swede. By permission of the poet. / 147 "Conversation" by Buson from *Haiku* translated by R. H. Blyth. By permission of The Hokuseido Press. / 147 "That duck, bobbing up" by Joso from *Cricket Songs Japanese Haiku* translated by Henry Behn. ©1992 Prescott Behn, Pamela Behn Adam, an Peter Behn. By permission of Marian Reiner. / 149 "the visitor" from *sca poems for rotten kids* by sean o huigan. By permission of Black Moss Pres / 150 "Purple Cow" from *An Armadillow is not a Pillow* by Lois Simmie ©1986. By permission of Greystone Books, a Division of Douglas & McIntyre. / 152, 153 "Grass Song" and "Let's Sing of Strawberries" fr *Wind In My Pocket* by Ellen Bryan Obed (Breakwater Books, 1990). T ©1990 Ellen Bryan Obed. Illustrations ©Shawn Steffler . By permiss the author and the publisher. / 155 "The Snowflake" by Walter de Mare. By permission of the Literary Trustees of Walter de la Mare, Society of Authors as their representative. / 156 "Hurricane" by D Brand. From *Earth Magic*, © 1979 by Dionne Brand. / 156 "Cold S Monica Kulling. ©1998 by Monica Kulling. By permission of Mari Reiner for the author. / 158 "Fame Was a Claim of Uncle Ed's" fro *Laughing Out Loud* by Ogden Nash. ©1941 by Ogden Nash. By pe of Little, Brown and Company. / 158 "I Left My Head" from *See Poison Ivy* by Lilian Moore. ©1975 Lilian Moore. By permission o Reiner for the author.

Photo Credits

6-7 Susan Ashukian Photography; 15 China Tourism Press/Image R 24, 26 Free Spirit Publishing Inc.; 25 Arlene Erlback; 54 John Lawrence/Tony Stone Images; 66 Hulton Getty Picture Collections, Stone Images; 67 Tony Stone Images; 72-73 (background) *NASA*; FPG/Masterfile; 74-75 (background) ©Imtek Imagineering/Maste James Balog/Tony Stone Images; 89 Tom Walker/Tony Stone Im 93 (background) ©Bill and Sally Fletcher/Tom Stack & Associat ("The Little Dipper," The constellation Cassiopeia," "The co Cygnus, the Swan," "The constellation Bootes") Hansen Plar Publications; 94-95 (background) Corel Stock Photo Library; ' (background) Kennan Ward Photography; 97 (star chart) Kid 119 Everett Collection, Inc., New York, NY; 151 Dave Starrett Photography; 154 Dept of Dev/Tourism Gov't of Nfld & Lab/l John Byrne.

Illustrations

6 Vicky Elsom; 22, 139 Steve Attoe; 29, 66, 77 Dan Hobbs; 3 142 Dayle Dodwell; 45 Barbara Spurll; 56-57 Tomio Nitto; 9 Davies Leclair/Visual Sense; 102-103 Martin Springett; 111 Bathurst; 144-145 Daphne McCormick

Cornerstones Development Team

HERE ARE THE PEOPLE WHO WORKED HARD TO MAKE THIS BOOK EXCITING FOR YOU!

WRITING TEAM

Christine McClymont
Patrick Lashmar
Dennis Strauss
Patricia FitzGerald-Chesterman
Cam Colville
Robert Cutting
Stephen Hurley
Luigi Iannacci
Oksana Kuryliw
Caroline Lutyk

GAGE EDITORIAL

Joe Banel
Caroline Cobham
Rivka Cranley
Elizabeth Long
David MacDonald
Evelyn Maksimovich
Darleen Rotozinski
Carol Waldock

GAGE PRODUCTION

Anna Kress
Bev Crann

DESIGN, ART DIRECTION & ELECTRONIC ASSEMBLY

Pronk&Associates

ADVISORY TEAM

Connie Fehr Burnaby SD, BC
Elizabeth Sparks Delta SD, BC
Joan Alexander St. Albert PSSD, AB
Carol Germyn Calgary B of E, AB
Cathy Sitko Edmonton Catholic SD, AB
Laura Haight Saskatoon SD, SK
Linda Nosbush Prince Albert SD, SK
Maureen Rodniski Winnipeg SD, MB
Cathy Saytar Dufferin-Peel CDSB, ON
Jan Adams Thames Valley DSB, ON
Linda Ross Thames Valley DSB, ON
John Cassano York Region DSB, ON
Carollynn Desjardins Nipissing-Parry Sound CDSB, ON
Dave Hodgkinson Waterloo Region DSB, ON
Michelle Longlade Halton CDSB, ON
Sharon Morris Toronto CDSB, ON
Heather Sheehan Toronto CDSB, ON
Ruth Scott Brock University, ON
Elizabeth Thorn Nipissing University, ON
Jane Abernethy Chipman & Fredericton SD, NB
Darlene Whitehouse-Sheehan Chipman & Fredericton SD, NB
Carol Chandler Halifax Regional SB, NS
Martin MacDonald Strait Regional SB, NS
Ray Doiron University of PEI, PE
Robert Dawe Avalon East SD, NF
Margaret Ryall Avalon East SD, NF

Contents

Oh, Joyous House

Poem by Richard Janzen, age 12

When I walk home from school,
I see many houses
Many houses down many streets.
They are warm, comfortable houses
But other people's houses
I pass without much notice.

Then as I walk farther, farther
I see a house, the house.
It springs up with a jerk
That speeds my pace; I lurch forward.
Longing makes me happy, I bubble inside.
It's my house.

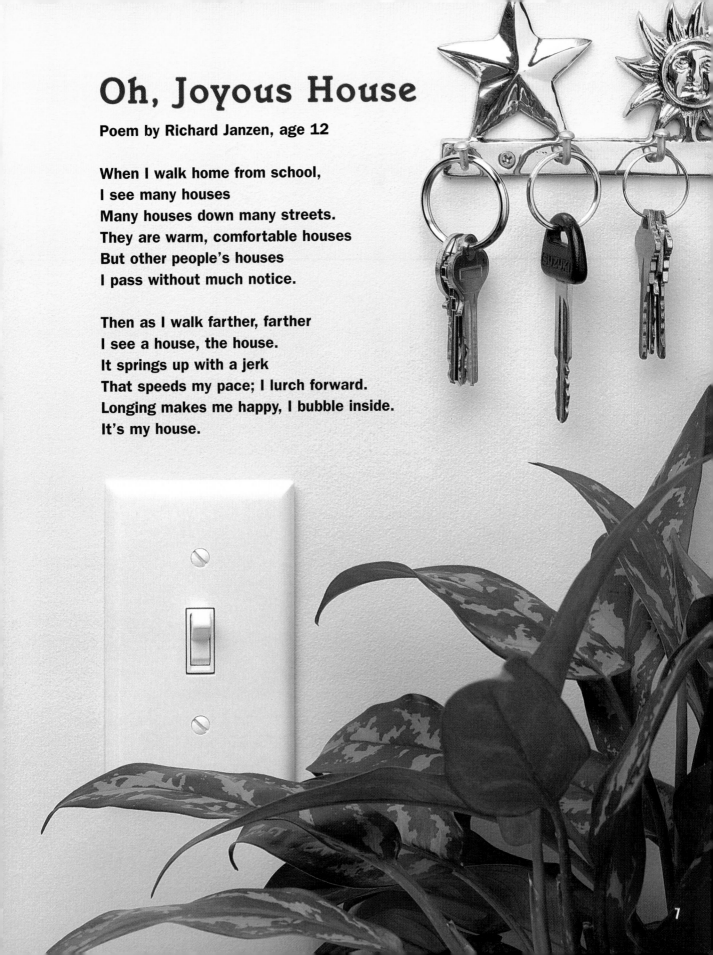

**BEFORE
READING**

The story *Roses Sing on New Snow* takes place in Vancouver about 100 years ago. Read on to find out why it has such an interesting title!

THE NEW WORLD
Often, immigrants from Asia and Europe called Canada and the United States the "New World," and their homeland the "Old World."

Story by
Paul Yee

Pictures by
Harvey Chan

Roses Sing on New Snow

Seven days a week, every week of the year, Maylin cooked in her father's restaurant. It was a spot well known throughout the New World for its fine food.

But when compliments and tips were sent to the chef, they never reached Maylin because her father kept the kitchen door closed and told everyone that it was his two sons who did all the cooking.

Maylin's father and brothers were fat and lazy from overeating, for they loved food.

But a well-cooked meal would always make them smile.
So Maylin worked to renew their spirits and used only the best
ingredients in her cooking.

Maylin loved food too, but for different reasons.
To Chinatown came men lonely and cold and bone-tired.
Their families and wives waited in China.

Then one day it was announced that the governor of South
China was coming to town. For a special banquet, each
restaurant in Chinatown was invited to bring its best dish.

Maylin's father ordered her to spare no expense and to use
all her imagination on a new dish. She shopped in the market
for fresh fish and knelt in her garden for herbs and greens.

In no time she had fashioned a dish of delectable flavours and aromas, which she named Roses Sing on New Snow.

Maylin's father sniffed happily and went off to the banquet, dressed in his best clothes and followed by his two sons.

Now the governor also loved to eat. His eyes lit up like lanterns at the array of platters that arrived. Every kind of meat, every colour of vegetable, every bouquet of spices was present. His chopsticks dipped eagerly into every dish.

When he was done, he pointed to Maylin's bowl and said, "That one wins my warmest praise! It reminded me of China, and yet it transported me far beyond. Tell me, who cooked it?"

Maylin's father waddled forward and repeated the lie he had told so often before. "Your Highness, it was my two sons who prepared it."

"Is that so?" The governor stroked his beard thoughtfully. "Then show my cook how the dish is done. I will present it to my emperor in China and reward you well!"

Maylin's father and brothers rushed home. They burst into the kitchen and forced Maylin to list all her ingredients. Then they made her demonstrate how she had chopped the fish and carved the vegetables and blended the spices.

They piled everything into huge baskets and then hurried back.

A stove was set up before the governor and his cook. Maylin's brothers cut the fish and cleaned the vegetables and ground the spices. They stoked a fire and cooked the food. But with one taste, the governor threw down his chopsticks.

"You impostors! Do you take me for a fool?" he bellowed. "That is not Roses Sing on New Snow!"

Maylin's father tiptoed up and peeked. "Why ... why, there is one spice not here," he stuttered.

"Name it and I will send for it!" roared the impatient governor.

But Maylin's father had no reply, for he knew nothing about spices.

Maylin's older brother took a quick taste and said, "Why, there's one vegetable missing!"

"Name it, and my men will fetch it!" ordered the governor.

But no reply came, for Maylin's older brother knew nothing about food.

Maylin's older brother blamed the fishmonger. "He gave us the wrong kind of fish!" he cried.

"Then name the right one, and my men will fetch it!" said the governor.

Again there was no answer.

Maylin's father and brothers quaked with fear and fell to their knees. When the governor pounded his fist on the chair, the truth quickly spilled out. The guests were astounded to hear that a woman had cooked this dish. Maylin's father hung his head in shame as the governor sent for the real cook.

Maylin strode in and faced the governor and his men. "Your Excellency, you cannot take this dish to China!" she announced.

"What?" cried the governor. "You dare refuse the emperor a chance to taste this wonderful creation?"

"This is a dish of the New World," Maylin said. "You cannot recreate it in the Old."

But the governor ignored her words and scowled. "I can make your father's life miserable here," he threatened her. So she said, "Let you and I cook side by side, so you can see for yourself."

The guests gasped at her daring request. However, the governor nodded, rolled up his sleeves, and donned an apron. Together, Maylin and the governor cut and chopped. Side by side they heated two woks, and then stirred in identical ingredients.

When the two dishes were finally finished, the governor took a taste from both. His face paled, for they were different.

"What is your secret?" he demanded. "We selected the same ingredients and cooked side by side!"

"If you and I sat down with paper and brush and black ink, could we bring forth identical paintings?" asked Maylin.

From that day on Maylin was renowned in Chinatown as a great cook and a wise person. Her fame even reached as far as China.

But the emperor, despite the governor's best efforts, was never able to taste the most delicious New World dish, nor to hear Roses Sing on New Snow. ◗

FOLLOW UP

Do you think *Roses Sing on New Snow* is a good title for this story? Which senses does it appeal to (sight, sound, touch, smell, taste)? Be ready to explain your answers!

Did You Know

- The first Chinese immigrants came to British Columbia during the Gold Rush.

- Then, 100 years ago, many Chinese men came to Canada to build the railways.

- If they were married, their wives and families stayed in China and the men sent money back home.

Understanding the Story

Recipe for Fame

- Why do you think Maylin's father told people his sons did all the cooking in his restaurant?
- The governor from South China called the father and his sons "impostors." What did he mean?
- Why do you think the governor could not cook Roses Sing on New Snow as well as Maylin?
- What do you predict will be the next step in Maylin's career?

Imagine!

Invent your own recipe for Roses Sing on New Snow. Set up a class display of all your recipes.

"New World" Family

CLASS DISCUSSION

It's puzzling: Why wouldn't Maylin's father give her any credit for her cooking? Did he think boys were more important than girls? Why do you think he felt that way? In Canada today, most people believe boys and girls, and mothers and fathers, are equally important. With your class, talk about some of the ways that family values have changed since the days of *Roses Sing on New Snow*.

Viewing – Chinese Painting

Maylin mentions painting with "paper and brush and black ink." She's talking about Chinese brush painting — a beautiful traditional form of art.

Here is an example.

Compare Harvey Chan's illustrations with the traditional brush painting. Then try your own brush-and-ink painting.

Read about author Paul Yee on page 16.

Career Tip

If you think you would like to be a chef

- try eating different dishes from around the world

- learn to cook simple, dishes in your own kitchen

- after high school, take a college course in cooking

Meanwhile, enjoy good food!

MEET AUTHOR

Paul Yee

by Susan Hughes

"Writing is fun!" says Paul Yee. "It's like magic. From nothing comes a book to hold in my hands." Of course, a story doesn't really come from nothing. At his home in Toronto, Paul works hard at the craft of writing. He spends lots of time thinking and making notes.

He explores his memories, too — the experiences he had growing up in Vancouver's Chinatown, and the family stories his aunt used to tell. All these things spark ideas for stories.

Many of Paul's stories are folk tales set in Canada's past. He is fascinated with the tales of the early Chinese immigrants who came to western Canada.

"I care about all those people who have gone before me. They made possible the world I live in. Today, the Chinese are accepted in North America, but it wasn't always like this. We owe a debt to those who paved the way."

Paul also says, "We can learn a lot from the people who lived ordinary lives — maybe just as much as we can learn from generals or politicians."

As you can see, Paul is hooked on history. He studied history at university. But he soon returned to Chinatown to learn about the early history of his community. He wanted to rediscover his roots.

As a writer, Paul wants to make history come alive for young readers of today. He feels that kids are grabbed by history when it is presented to them through a terrific story. "They are fascinated by it. And they remember it!" he adds.

In 1990, Paul published a popular collection of stories about Chinese immigrants to Canada. It is called *Tales from Gold Mountain: Stories of the Chinese in the New World.* Our story, *Roses Sing on New Snow: A Delicious Tale,* was published as a separate picture book.

"Many of the early Chinese immigrants to Canada were men," Paul reminds us. "They worked and sent money home. Eventually most of them went home themselves. But there were some women here too! So I wanted to write a story with a strong female character.

"The problem was, I wanted to be true to the past. I tried to think of a place in which a female could naturally have a strong position. That ended up being the kitchen," explains Paul.

Maylin is a cook in her father's New World restaurant. She creates a fabulous dish, "Roses Sing on New Snow." But don't ask the author for the recipe. Maylin knows it. But not Paul. "It's one of those chef's secrets!" he laughs.

Paul is pleased that his tales appeal to young people. "I think it's the surprises they like — the quirkiness of my tales."

Paul has some advice for young writers. He suggests they choose subjects they feel strongly about. "Writing takes a lot of time and energy. You're more likely to stick at it, if it's something you really care about."

And writing is something that Paul had decided to stick with. In 1991, he decided to write full-time. So knock on his door any morning and you'll find him in sweat pants and a T-shirt. He might be in the kitchen rereading what he wrote the day before. He might be in the living room jotting down ideas with paper and pen. Or you could find him in the study, sitting at the computer. He heads for the keyboard when he is ready to put it all together—and write.

"I like making history last longer," Paul says. He continues to preserve history through his stories for young people.

A PIONEER FAMILY

THE ROBERTSONS

LIZZIE   MEG AND TOMMY   GEORGE   PA ROBERTSON   MA ROBERTSON   SARAH   GRANNY   WILLY

BEFORE READING

How long ago was 1840? You would have to go back in time at least six generations, to when your great-great-great-great-grandparents lived. Read on to see what family life was like then.

Article by
Barbara Greenwood

Pictures by
Heather Collins

MEET THE ROBERTSONS, a pioneer family living on a backwoods farm in eastern Canada in 1840. Although the Robertsons are a made-up family, their struggle to clear the forest, to plant, to harvest, and to make a good life for themselves echoes the efforts of our early settlers, who worked hard to build a home, a community, and a country.

The Robertsons, like real-life settlers, live by this motto:

> *Eat it up,*
> *Wear it out,*
> *Make it do,*
> *Or go without.*

The Robertson children learn early that "many hands make light work" and that it's best to "make hay while the sun shines." But life isn't all chores and making do. Maple-sugar frolics and harvest suppers, husking bees and barn dances, the birth of lambs and the search for a honey tree brighten the days as the seasons pass from winter to spring, from summer to fall.

INSIDE THE LOG HOUSE

Work must have seemed never-ending to the early settlers. Every pair of hands was needed to keep the family fed and clothed. Inside the house the women prepared the big meal of the day, which was eaten at noon.

Mrs. Robertson lifts a loaf of bread out of the bake kettle. Early that morning she had put the dough (which had risen overnight) into the kettle and settled it among the coals to bake.

Sarah (ten years old) helps wind the yarn. She also gives the cradle a rock whenever baby Tommy cries.

A small storeroom holds two barrels of salted pork, a basket of potatoes (covered to keep them from freezing), a barrel of salt, and pots and pans not needed for today's meal.

Next year, Lizzie (four years old) will start doing simple chores such as setting the table or helping to dry the dishes.

Granny spins sheep's wool into yarn on the spinning wheel she brought with her from Scotland.

Meg (fifteen years old) mixes flour and water to make dumplings. She will drop the dumplings into the stew bubbling over the fire.

George (thirteen years old) and Willy (nine years old) sleep in the loft on straw ticks laid directly on the floor.

The barn is used for storing grain and hay or grass for the animals. There is a small stable for the family's oxen and milk cows. Behind the barn, on the warm, south side, is a shelter for sheep.

Stones cleared from the fields will be used to make the cellar walls of the new house.

The bake oven is used in good weather. In winter, Mrs. Robertson bakes indoors in a kettle.

Sarah bangs on a pot with a spoon to call everyone in for the noon meal.

Mr. Robertson will haul the logs he has cut to the sawmill, where they will be sawn into boards for the Robertsons' new house.

This shanty was the very first shelter the family built. Now it is used as a workshop. Almost everything on a backwoods farm has to be made by hand: furniture, sleds, cupboards, animal pens.

A pail of lye is kept in the privy. Once a day a cupful is thrown down the hole to keep the odour tolerable.

Willy and George haul water for the family and the animals. Next they will split wood for the fire.

Does pioneer family life remind you of camping? In what ways? Pioneers had to do everything themselves — with some help from friends and neighbours.

Past and Present – Make a Chart

A Pioneer Family describes more than a dozen chores done by members of the Robertson family. Make a chart to compare pioneer chores, both indoor and outdoor, with the way we do those jobs today.

Past: Pioneer Chores	Present: The Modern Way
1. cooking on a wood stove	– we cook on an electric stove
2. winding yarn	– I help my mom wind the yarn for her knitting
3. rocking the cradle	
4. spinning wool into yarn	
5. baking bread	

Imagine!
Think about life before cars and electricity. Then design a poster called "Five things I Like About Pioneer Days!"

A Motto to Live By

Choose a partner. Reread the Robertson's "motto to live by."

**Eat it up,
Wear it out,
Make it do,
Or go without.**

Discuss with your partner what each line means. Then think about it: Would this be a good motto for cutting down on waste and saving money? Do you think you and your family could live by this motto?

Make a

JUMPING JACK

By Barbara Greenwood

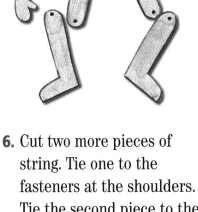

You can make a jumping jack just like Willy's. How good are you at understanding directions? Read all the steps and picture yourself doing each one before you start making it.

You will need

- tracing paper
- a pencil
- scissors
- sticky tape
- heavy cardboard
- markers or crayons
- a small nail
- 6 brass paper fasteners
- string

1. Draw the body parts you see at the top of the page on the cardboard. Your drawings can be much bigger than the ones shown, but try to draw similar shapes. Cut out the cardboard pieces.

2. Colour in clothing and a face.

3. Use a small nail to punch holes in the places shown by the black dots.

4. Use the paper fasteners to attach the arms and legs to the body.

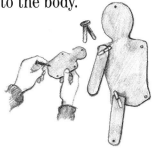

5. Cut one piece of string long enough to make a loop. Thread it through the top of the head and knot it.

6. Cut two more pieces of string. Tie one to the fasteners at the shoulders. Tie the second piece to the fasteners at the hips.

7. Tie another piece of string to the shoulder and hip strings. Let the tail of the string hang free.

8. To work the jumping jack, hold it by the loop on the head and pull the hanging string. The arms and legs will jump and flex.

(left to right) Klaudia, mother, grandmother, David

FAMILIES *Today*

Klaudia —
"My grandmother lives with us."

Personal Account as told to **Arlene Erlbach**

"I'm the only child in a house with lots of adults, so I get lots of attention. I live with my mom, my grandmother, my Uncle Mark, and my cousin David. I love living with all of them— and living in North America. I was five when my mother and I moved here from Poland.

"My grandmother was living here and told us how nice it was. So my mother and I came to visit. Then we decided to make arrangements to stay. I love it here. There are so many shops with items to buy.

"My mother and I go in-line skating together often. She's very good at it. For a few years, we acted in a Polish theatre group together. My mother does more things with me than most mothers do with their kids, so I'm very fortunate.

"I'm also very close to my grandmother. She doesn't go on trips with my mother and me. She's afraid to fly. She doesn't skate, either. My grandmother loves to cook, and I like to help her with the cooking. Last night we made blueberry kolachkies. Kolachkies are filled cookies that are very popular in Poland. On Sundays, I almost always help her cook the meal. That's a special day for us. My mom, cousin, uncle, grandmother, and I all have dinner together."

Tam — "I'm adopted."

. . . .

Personal Account as told to
Aylette Jenness

"I have a big family. Ari and Chessie aren't adopted, but the rest of us are. We were adopted when we were babies.

"When someone in our family has a birthday, they get to pick out a dinner that they want, and they open presents at the end of the meal. Sometimes we buy the presents, and sometimes we make them. Everyone gets a lot of presents!"

Tam's mother says that, from time to time, Tasha, Kri, and Tam have asked the questions that adopted children often ask: "Where did I come from? Who was my mother?" She explains that they were born to another woman. As they grow older, she talks about their ethnic backgrounds. But she emphasizes that she is their mother, their parent.

"A parent is a person who takes care of you, raises you, looks after you, and loves you," she says. And that's what she and her husband are for Tasha, Kri, and Tam, just as they are for Ari and Chessie.

Kri (on left swing), Tam, Mom, Ari, Dad,
Tasha (sitting), Chessie (On right swing)

Aaron's dad (top), Aaron (left), Randy (right), mom (holding Arnie, the dog)

Randy and Aaron — "We're stepbrothers."

Personal Account as told to
Arlene Erlbach

Randy: "I have a stepdad, regular dad, mom, and a stepbrother named Aaron. Aaron is three weeks younger than I am, so I think of him as my younger brother. Of course he's not a little brother.

"My mother got divorced when I was about three years old. I don't remember what it was like when my biological dad and mom lived together.

"I've always known Aaron and his dad. Aaron's mom died when Aaron was three. About a year later, my mom started dating Aaron's father.

"When my mom started dating Aaron's dad, I didn't think about it much. But when I heard that they were getting married and I'd have a brother, that seemed weird. I'd never had a brother before, so I didn't know what it would be like. I didn't know what it would be like having a stepdad either.

"Aaron can be very helpful. He's good at math and helps me with it. I'm not as good at math as he is. I'm a better reader, though. Aaron is better at helping out around the house and keeping his room neat. My mom says we're complete opposites, and she's right about that.

"My stepdad and my real dad are complete opposites, too. My real dad likes to play sports with me, like baseball and basketball. I see him on Tuesdays and every other weekend. He yells when he gets mad. My stepdad is quiet and never yells at me or Aaron. He's a psychologist. I can talk to him about things I may not want to discuss with other people. He's a very understanding type of adult."

Aaron: "I usually like having a stepbrother. Randy has his group of friends, and I have my group of friends. So having a stepbrother gives me a chance to know lots of different people. I like it when all of us play Sega and basketball together.

"I like it at night when Randy and I watch TV together, too. Our favourites are "The Simpsons" and sports. It's fun to watch programs and have somebody my age to talk about them with.

"My stepmom can be really nice. She'll take me and Randy places, like the movies or the mall. She makes good things to eat, like pizza and spaghetti.

"I have a feeling my real mom would have gotten madder at me when I didn't do chores or acted silly and noisy. Still, I wish I could still be with her. But I usually feel fortunate to have my stepmom for a stepmother.

"Randy is close to my dad, but I don't mind sharing him. Every morning at 6:30, my dad and I have breakfast together alone. We talk privately. My dad teaches me things, like how to do algebra.

"I don't really know Randy's dad very well. I don't see him, since Randy goes to visit him at his place. I guess it's good that Randy and I have a regular break from each other. We have some time apart — and the house is quieter." ◆

FOLLOW UP

Did you learn anything new about families from the article? Which of the families in the article is most like yours? Which is most different?

Congratulations! You're becoming an expert on families!

Understanding the Article

Getting to Know You

- Klaudia has an unusual family. Why does she enjoy living in her family?

- Tam is an adopted child, but she feels just the same as her non-adopted sisters. How does her mother help her to feel this way?

- How do Randy and Aaron feel about being stepbrothers and having stepparents?

- What is a family today? Work with a partner. Start with the phrase, "A family is ..."

Family Vocabulary — Nouns and Compound Words

Brother	Sister
○ Grandfather	_____
Grandson	_____
○ Aunt	_____
Stepmother	_____
Stepsister	_____
○ Nephew	_____
Father-in-law	_____

In your notebook, complete the chart with words that describe family members. All of these words are called **nouns.** Remember: nouns are the names of people, places, or things. Some of the nouns are **compound words** – two words put together. Can you find them?

Add as many family words as you can!

Create a Family Album

Collect photographs of people in your family, or make your own drawings. Then arrange them in a scrapbook or photo album. For each family member, compose a caption. Here are some examples:

Something To Think About!

In all the families in the article, parents and children help each other out. What are some examples? How do you and your family help each other?

A Greeting Card

YOUR TURN TO WRITE

Do you have relatives who live in another city or country? Who would you like to send a message to? Make a greeting card that says "Hello!" Write a short message about what you're up to. Then pop it into an envelope with a photo of yourself. Address it, add a stamp, and mail it. Your relative will be thrilled to receive it!

What is a miracle?
Read this story to
find out about one
special kind of
miracle.

CALL IT A
Miracle

Story by
Anne Carter

Pictures by
Renée Mansfield

MONDAY

MONDAY

I don't know what to do about my mom.

Monday mornings are the worst. First I hear her alarm clock rriinngg!

I stay out of the way and wait for the crash. She always drops it.

"Mom," I whisper. "You have to get up."

From under the covers, she groans. "I hate going in to work this early."

"You'll be late for work. Mr. High N. Mighty will be mad at you." Mr. High N. Mighty is Mom's boss.

"I'll get out the cereal," I say. "But you have to promise to get up."

This works.

Mom calls this "bribery." I just call it breakfast.

TUESDAY

TUESDAY

I still don't know what to do about my mom.

Tuesday morning she won't get dressed for work.

"I hate high heels and those scratchy suits." All her clothes come flying out of the closet. "Why can't I wear running shoes and my old, fuzzy sweatshirt?"

I've been downtown to Mom's office. Nobody wears playclothes. Especially Mr. High N. Mighty. He looks so uncomfortable, he never sits down.

I pick out pants and a top from the pile on the floor. "Try this. It's soft and it matches."

This works.

Mom calls this "conforming." I just call it getting dressed.

WEDNESDAY

Things aren't getting any better.

Wednesday morning she says she can't stand eating lunch downtown.

"Why eat in crowded restaurants with strangers? I want to eat lunch at home with you."

I make her a peanut butter and beansprout sandwich just the way she likes it. I pack it with a heart-shaped chocolate in the top of her briefcase.

This works.

Mom calls this a "compromise." I just call it lunch.

WEDNESDAY

THURSDAY

Things are definitely worse.

Thursday at school, I get called to the office. There's a phone call for me...it's my mom.

"I left a big file at home. Mr. High N. Mighty will kill me," she wails. She always has homework. She works on her "files" long after I've gone to bed. Sometimes in the morning, I find her asleep at her desk, her head resting on a pillow of paper.

It's hard to remember things if you don't get a good night's sleep.

"Lock your door," I suggest. "Put a 'Keep Out' sign on it. You'll find the file tonight and then take it in tomorrow."

This works.

Mom calls this "lying low." I just call it hide-and-seek.

FRIDAY

She's driving me crazy. Friday morning she won't get in the car.

"That drive is too stressful and a total waste of time. An hour through traffic to get to work and another hour back home again."

I roll up my sleeves. I show her my watch. "You just wasted twenty minutes. I'm going to be late for school. Do you want me to...**get in trouble**?"

This works.

Mom calls this a "threat." I just call it telling time.

SATURDAY

SATURDAY

I think we're heading for a black hole in outer space.

Saturday morning, Mr. High N. Mighty phones. He needs Mom at work.

"But it's a beautiful, sunny Saturday. I wanted to take you biking in the park."

I find the book Mom gave me for my birthday called *One Hundred Things To Do On A Rainy Day*.

"It's OK Mom. I'll come with you and read my new book. We'll bike-ride tomorrow."

This works.

Mom calls this a "sacrifice." I just call it love.

SUNDAY

Help!

Sunday morning Mr. High N. Mighty phones again. I ask him to please wait.

"Mom, it's Mr. High N. Mighty. He says he needs your help for just an hour."

Mom dives under the covers. "Tell him your great aunt died. Tell him I died. Tell him it's the weekend and I want to stay home."

I talk again with Mr. High N. Mighty.

Mom's still a big bump under the covers. She's playing dead but I know better.

"I told him what you said."

The covers fly off the bed. "What!" she says. "You didn't really...*did you*?"

My Mom rushes to the phone. I've never seen her run so fast.

When she's finished talking, she shoots like a star across her bed.

"Yeessss!!!!" She shouts triumphantly. "We found a solution."

"He's going to bring me a computer and a fax machine so I can work at home sometimes. You and I can have lunch together. I won't have to dress up or drive downtown!"

I smile. Then I notice that her eyes are closing. "Mom, you better get up now," I say. "Mr. High N. Mighty told me he'd be here in fifteen minutes."

This works.

Mom calls it a "miracle."

And so do I. ◈

SUNDAY

FOLLOW UP

At the end of the story, Mom and the writer have solved their biggest problem. What was the problem, and how did they solve it? Why do you think they called their solution "a miracle"?

Role Reversal

What happens in this story is called "role reversal." This means that two people, for example, a student and a teacher, switch roles. One person starts acting the way the other person usually acts. Describe how role reversal works in this story.

In a group, brainstorm an idea for a TV show about role reversal. Present your idea to the class.

Have you heard this one?

"Johnny, get up! It's time for school."

"I don't want to, Mom."

"Hurry up, or you'll be late!"

"But Mom, I don't want to go to school today!"

"You have to, Johnny, you're the principal!"

Understanding the Story

What to do about Mom?

- Who is the practical person in this story — Mom or her son? Why do you think this?

- Does Mom care for her son as much as he cares for her? Explain.

- Do you think the boy's dad lives with them? Give reasons for your answer.

- What are your three favourite examples of humour in this story?

A Pattern Story

This story is based on a pattern — a problem for each day of the week. Make a story diagram of *Call It a Miracle* by filling in a calendar for one week. Now, write a funny pattern story of your own. You might choose the same pattern — days of the week. Or, invent your own pattern. Then write about how your family copes with problems such as:

- driving to the hockey arena at 5:00 a.m.
- getting everyone to sit together at dinner time
- choosing which television program to watch
- getting along with the babysitter

	Monday	Tuesday	Wednesday	Thursday	Friday	Saturday	Sunday
Problem							
Solution							

Mom's Big Words — Increase Your Vocabulary

Match the words in the left-hand column to the correct definition in the right-hand column. Write the correct number and letter together in your notebook.

1. bribery
2. conforming
3. compromise
4. lying low
5. threat
6. sacrifice
7. miracle

a) hiding; staying out of the way to avoid trouble

b) a promise to hurt or punish someone

c) offering a person a gift to get him/her to do something wrong

d) giving up something important to help someone else

e) following the rules, or acting the same as others

f) an amazing happening that cannot be easily explained

g) both sides give up something to reach an agreement

Student Poems

Pictures by
Philippe Béha

Mad

Poem by Beth Tossell, Grade 4

I feel mad when my little brother
knocks over a chair and pulls
the tablecloth down, just for
the fun of it,
when I leave my shoes outside
in a storm, and they get
soaking wet,
and when my parents wake me
up when I'm deeply
asleep.

Glad to Be Alive

Poem by Capricia Quick,
Grade 4

"When you were born,"
my mother said, "you were
a beautiful baby.
I loved to hear you cry. I cried
with you. I was
so glad you were alive.
I didn't know what I would do
without you."

Forever and a Day

Poem by Heather Lachman, Grade 4

I want to go home.
The day is long.
It has been long ever since
I woke up.

YOUR TURN TO WRITE

A Family Poem

Family poems are all about...

feeling sad, mad, happy, blue
wanting to stay, to go, to cry, to fly
people you care about,
who care about you.

The words can be simple, if the feelings are true.

To write your own poem:

1. Start with one of the first lines the student poets used (or make up your own).

   "I want to go home..."
   "I feel mad when..."
   "When you were born..."

2. Write down all your ideas and feelings without worrying about choosing the right words.

3. Go over your ideas and pick the most interesting ones. Organize these into lines to make a poem.

4. Read your poem aloud to yourself. If you think of some better words, change them!
   Poets work hard to polish their poems.

5. You might post your poem on the refrigerator for everyone to read.

BEFORE READING

When Grandma died, she left Joyce a special gift. Read the story to find out what the gift was, and how it helped Joyce's whole family.

La Ronge: a town in northern Saskatchewan

In the Garden

Story by Carolyn Marie Mamchur with Meguido Zola
Pictures by Brian Deines

When Grandma died, she gave me a handkerchief — a plain white cotton handkerchief with small blue flowers around the edge. "Forget-me-nots," my mother said.

The handkerchief was tied in a knot. It came in a tiny crackerjack box...without any crackerjack in it. That's what my grandma gave me.

Grandma gave my brother her coin collection. Some of those coins came from a time before anybody even knew what a reserve was, before there were TVs, before Coke in bottles, before ripple chips and unemployment cheques — at least that's how my uncle put it.

Anyway, I know it was a long time ago; and those coins were probably worth a fortune.

Grandma gave my older sister all her scarves. My grandma loved scarves and had plenty. One had silver threads running through it. I used to play with that scarf every time I visited Grandma. We would go out into her garden and she would tie her hair up in a scarf. And so would I...the scarf with the silver threads in it, the one my sister got.

But me, I got a white handkerchief with blue forget-me-nots around the border.

The night after the prayer service, I took the handkerchief out of the crackerjack box. I took it to bed, tucked in the sleeve of my sweatshirt.

The hanky smelled like Grandma, when she was working in the garden. Like earth, and nuts, and fresh water from a deep lake north of La Ronge.

In the night, when I was missing my grandma more than I could stand, I took out the handkerchief and gave it a little squeeze.

It still had the knot in it. Inside the knot I felt something. I rubbed the hanky between my fingers. Something inside the hanky was moving, something small and hard and gritty — like sand.

I got up and went to the window. I opened the hanky very carefully and spread it out on the windowsill. Inside the hanky were tiny black seeds — hundreds and hundreds of them. I tied them back into my hanky and went to sleep.

When I woke up, it was late; it was even past lunchtime. I found my mother out back arguing with my brother. He wanted to sell the coins to buy a bike. My mom said no.

It was then I made my announcement.

"I'm planting a garden," I said.

"Where?" my mother wanted to know.

"Out there," I pointed to our backyard. Our backyard's full of cars that won't go and couch grass.

"Oh sure," my mom said.

"I am!" I insisted, stupid tears juicing up in my eyes.

"It takes time to grow a garden," my mother explained. Her eyes were getting juicy, too. "More time than we'll have. Come the end of summer, your dad usually gets laid off. We'll have to move. You'll plant that garden for nothing. If it grows, you'll just have to leave it all behind. Don't bother. The city is no place for a garden."

I knew enough about gardens to know that couch grass was no good for it.

Sister Loretta, my grade four teacher, told me how to dig

couch grass. And how to sift the dirt through a sieve so that none of the small roots would escape and grow again.

It took weeks. I didn't have a real sieve. I used a piece of screen from my bedroom window—it was broken anyway. It worked great.

One night my mom came out and helped me.

"Aren't you getting tired?" she wanted to know.

"No," I said. "I feel like Grandma," I told her.

We worked until it was too dark to see where we had dug.
I think I sieved the same spot three times. It felt good.

Finally, I planted Grandma's seeds.

I watered and weeded and watched and waited, until, at last,
beans popped out of the ground. Grasslike shoots formed a long
ribbon of pale green against the brown earth — carrots. My garden
had begun to grow.

My parsnips got fat. I tied strings around my cauliflowers so they
wouldn't go yellow. I tied bits of rag on the tomato plants to keep
the birds away. And blue forgot-me-nots grew around everything,
a perfect border of tiny blue flowers.

Then, my favourite part: it was almost time to harvest, to eat
everything.

We'd already had a few baby carrots and enough tomatoes for
sandwiches.

Now, I wanted enough to store in the basement. I wanted
canned beet pickles and carrots dipped in wax to keep them firm all
winter. Mrs. Fitzpatrick did it that way, her daughter told me. It was
the way the Irish did things. And it was what I wanted, too.

August 28th, it happened. The hotel where my dad worked as a parking lot attendant went on strike. Everyone was out of work. Not just the maids, who were mostly Métis, like us, but **everybody** who worked there: cooks, bartenders, bellhops, carpenters, plumbers, even accountants for gosh's sake, **everybody.**

"I guess we'll be moving soon," my mom said, her voice full of that gritty, tired sound none of us liked.

"I should stick with the strikers," my dad said.

"How will that help?" my mom wanted to know: "What for?"

"We should stick together," my dad insisted.

"They don't care if you stay," my mom said. And she went to bed early.

The strike lasted a month.

Then, one day, my dad came in awful quiet, like he was terribly tired or had a bad toothache.

We were harvesting my vegetables. My sister was melting wax. My brother was hacking the cabbage. My mother was slicing beets for pickling. I was supervising, watching that everything was going just right. It was exciting.

"I'm not going back," he confessed. "I guess we shouldn't have hung around. We'll leave Monday."

My brother dropped a whole cabbage in the slop pail. My sister turned off the wax.

"There's no strike money left!" Dad yelled. "What can I do? Me? A migratory worker with no bank account." He threw his big boots across the linoleum. My mom left them there. She didn't say anything.

"Let's make some soup." Mom said after a bit. "Grandmother Rigadelle always made soup on a rainy day." I didn't tell Mom it wasn't raining. I guess she didn't notice.

She just wanted to do something.

It is true Grandma believed in the healing powers of soup.

My mom started peeling carrots and chopping celery and simmering chicken necks.

And then the idea came to me. We carried the pots of steaming vegetable soup in the trunk of my uncle's blue 1967 Chevy. He drove real slow so none of it would spill.

We served it to the strikers in paper cups we bought at the corner store — my uncle paid for them himself.

The strikers patted my dad on the back. They made slurpy smiling noises and complimented my mom.

"My little girl grew these vegetables," my dad announced. "Joyce, my younger daughter: she grew them in her garden. All by herself, she grew them — my younger daughter, Joyce." His voice was proud. "She's eleven, next January," Dad smiled.

The strikers clapped. All those tired, hungry people clapped.

And I clapped too. 🞔

FOLLOW UP

●

What was
Grandma's special
gift? How did the
gift grow and grow?

Imagine!
**You've been invited to write the
next chapter of this story for
a kids' magazine. But hurry,
the deadline is next week!**

Understanding the Story

Tending the Garden

❧ How did Joyce feel at first about the gift Grandma
gave her?

❧ When did Joyce realize she loved gardening, just like
her grandmother?

❧ Why was the strike a big problem for Joyce's dad and
the family?

❧ How did Joyce help her dad and the strikers?

❧ What do you think will happen next to Joyce and
her family?

Media Link

Three-Part Stories

We asked Carolyn Mamchur how she
planned her story. She told us she thinks
of it as having three parts.

PART 1, THE SET-UP: "In this part, I
introduced the main character, Joyce,
and explained what she wanted to
do."

PART 2, PROBLEMS: "In this part, I put
problems in Joyce's way – both people
and things. I ended this part with the
biggest problem of all."

PART 3, THE SOLUTION: "Finally, I
explained how Joyce solved her
problems. I also wanted to show how
she had grown and changed."

Carolyn says many stories follow this
three-part pattern. She said it works
for movies, too. Next time you watch
a movie, see if it follows this pattern:

PART 1: the first 20 minutes

PART 2: about an hour

PART 3: the last 20 minutes.

A *Special* Family Tree

Joyce inherited a love of gardening from her grandmother. Think about the folks in your family. What skills or attitudes might you have inherited from them? What new things would you like to learn from them?

Create a family tree with a difference. On the branches, write the names of family members. For each name, write something that person could teach you.

Mom
How to canoe

Pop
How to ride a horse

Cousin Maria
How to work with people

Uncle Zack
How to tell good jokes

My sister Ashley
How to paint pictures

Grandpa
How to speak Greek

BEFORE READING

Probably some of you — or your parents or grandparents — came to Canada from other countries. Share stories of other homelands with your classmates.

You Can Go Home Again

Story and Pictures by
Jirina Marton

WE HAVE NEVER had a day quite like this before. All afternoon the house was full of people celebrating freedom for my mom's old country. When I went to bed at night, I asked Mom to tell me a story about when she was little.

"Have I ever told you about Aunt Anna and Uncle Billy?" she asked.

"I loved going with my father to see them. The old house was like a fairy-tale setting. There were wonderful smells of old wood, books, spices, teas, and always cake as well.

"The house was full of mysterious things. Nearly all of them were brought back by Uncle Billy from his trips around the world. He was a concert pianist. But the house itself was unusual, too. There was a tiny elevator in one wall and it had a little door with a handle. It made incredible squeaking and rattling noises when food was sent up in it from the kitchen. I always imagined that at night dwarves would ride up and down in it so that they wouldn't have to climb the stairs."

"Did you ever hear Uncle Billy play?"

"Oh, often. Uncle Billy would sit down and play just for me. We would sit on the bench together and play 'four-handed.' My fingers were too short, but I felt so important.
He was such a patient teacher.

"But what I loved most were four shiny, dark, wooden elephants made of ebony. They were the only treasures I was allowed to play with... My aunt told lots of stories about them."

"What did you do with them?"
I wanted to know.

"Oh, I'd play school with them, or run races with them, or pretend that we were in the jungle. Sometimes I'd show them pictures from books, or I would just put the elephants on the windowsill and look out with them.

"Once I broke the left tusk off the biggest one. I was afraid that I wouldn't be allowed to play with them any more, but Father glued the tusk back on so carefully that you could hardly tell it had been broken."

I couldn't stop thinking about those elephants.

"Where are they now?" I asked Mom at breakfast the next day. She said she didn't know.

"Mom, you promised to finish the story," I said. Dad wanted to hear it, too.

"When the war started," Mom said, "Father, Aunt Anna, and Uncle Billy thought I would be safer out of the country. I didn't want to leave them, but I went. I was awfully homesick."

(Now if this happened to me, I wouldn't go.)

Mom told us that her aunt, her uncle, and even her dad died while she was away. Mom stopped. Dad put his hand over hers.

Then I had an idea.

"Maybe we can all go back to your city," I said, "and maybe I could play with those elephants. We could look for them." I thought Dad would say no, but he said it was "a thought worth looking into."

Soon after, we were on our way across the ocean in a big airplane. I wanted to stay awake and watch the clouds from the top, but I was too sleepy.

We landed in the morning and went to a small hotel. All afternoon long we walked through the big city.

We walked and walked. We crossed the river on an old bridge with statues. We visited big old churches.

Mom and Dad took lots of pictures. I took one of Mom and Dad in front of the house Mom lived in when she was small.

We visited the cemetery and went to Mom's old school.

People spoke a different language. They were all the same colour. But the children played hopscotch like we do.

The buildings were not as high as in Canada, except maybe the churches.

On the second day we went on the subway. I liked the long escalators.

"Where did Aunt and Uncle live? Could we go there?" I asked. Mom and Dad looked at each other, a little surprised. I guessed they had forgotten.

"Oh, dear, the elephants. I have no idea where they could be," Mom said, but we went anyway.

When we finally came to Aunt Anna's and Uncle Billy's house, Mom hardly recognized the place, and I was very disappointed, too. It was so different from what she had told me. The main hallway was dirty. The door to the little elevator was bricked over. Strangers lived there now.

"But have you seen the four elephants?" I asked the tenants. No one seemed to know what I was talking about.

We went to see nice places and people and I liked it all very much, but I kept thinking and asking people about the elephants, and no one had seen them.

I was upset when Dad said we would be leaving the next day. I knew that Mom was sad, too.

"Could we go back to Aunt's and Uncle's house one more time?" I asked. I begged. We went.

The house looked even worse in the dark. I sat down on the sidewalk, and I wanted to cry.

Dad put his hand on my shoulder. "Look, Annie," he said, "we know how important this is to you. The elephants are important to Mom and me as well. But you have done your best, and there just isn't anything else we can do to find them right now. I promise you we won't give up altogether. Let's get a bite to eat now, shall we?"

Right across from the house was a small restaurant. We went in.

That's when it happened. After I finished eating I looked up. I suddenly noticed something in a glass case on the wall.

"Mom, Dad!" I screamed. "The elephants are here! LOOK!"

The owner of the restaurant came out of the kitchen to see what the commotion was. Mom explained.

He gave Mom a long look and said, "I think I have a story for you."

We looked at him, surprised. I was so excited!

"I met your uncle first," he started. "I used to go to his concerts. Then one day he came here and I discovered that we were neighbours. Sometimes I would go and visit them during the war. Music helped us survive that strange, difficult time.

"The recipe for the dessert you just ate came from your aunt. She and your uncle often talked about you. They were so happy that you were safe.

"After your aunt died, your uncle came every day. He didn't want to be alone. He missed Anna so much... When the war ended, there was a short time of happiness. Then the new government confiscated your uncle's house and everything in it. They let him have just one room to live in.

"One evening he came over here. Under his coat he was carrying these elephants, wrapped in newspaper. He was sure that one day you would come back. So I promised him I would keep them safe for you as long as it would take, but I didn't really believe I would ever meet you!"

Then the owner went and unlocked the glass case and carefully took down the elephants. He set them on the table in front of Mom. She was crying, but I think they were sort of happy tears. She picked up the elephants and looked at them. The biggest had a line of glue on its tusk.

"Oh, Annie," said Mom, "if it hadn't been for you, we wouldn't have found them!" She hugged me, she hugged the owner, and Dad and I did too. We thanked him for everything and promised to come back. He waved to us.

Now, back home, I'm looking at the elephants. They have a special place in our house.

We'll never lose them again. ◉

FOLLOW UP

Where do you think Annie's mother felt most at home: in Canada, or in the old country? What about Annie?

Understanding the Story

Shiny Wooden Elephants

- What were Annie's mom's favourite memories of her childhood?

- Why did Annie want to visit her mom's home city?

- How did Annie's mom feel when the restaurant owner told her the story about how he got the elephants?

- Why were the elephants so important to both Annie and her mom?

- What do you think the title of the story means?

Imagine!
You live in Prague, and you want people to visit your city. So you design a travel poster. It lists three great reasons for visiting Prague!

Did You Know ?

For her story, Jirina Marton painted glowing images of Prague, the capital of the Czech Republic. It is a beautiful city and an ancient one —about 1000 years old. After World War II, the country became Communist. It won its freedom from the Soviet Union in 1989.

Family Treasures

When author Jirina Marton visited Prague, she read her story to Czech students. Their teacher asked them to think about this question:

If you were to return home after 30 years, what treasure would you most like to find?

Here is one student's answer. ▶

I have one big ceramic bird. It's very special to me because it has one of my favourite colours, blue. I would go find it even if it would be on the other side of the world. Sometimes I stare at it and I see it come alive or become very big. I would go find it because it's nice to keep such a memory. This parrot is my favourite ceramic thing in the house.

Peter

How would you answer the Czech teacher's question?
Write a paragraph about your favourite family keepsake.

MORE GOOD READING

Gregory Cool
by Caroline Binch
Gregory never wanted to visit his grandparents on their Caribbean island. No TV, no toys, no books. He complains about having nothing to do. Then he meets his cousin, who won't put up with "cool" Gregory. To his surprise, Gregory starts having fun. (a picture book)

🍁 *Ghost Train* **by Paul Yee**
Choon-yi, a talented brush painter, sails from China to join her father in North America. But when she arrives, she discovers he has died in a railroad accident. An amazing ride on a ghost train helps her to understand what really happened. (a picture book)

🍁 *The Killick: a Newfoundland story* **by Geoff Butler**
George and his grandfather sail to a deserted fishing outport. On the way home, they are caught in a fierce storm. Sheltering on an ice floe, the boy and the old man need all the courage they can find. This is a good story to read with an older friend. (a chapter-picture book)

🍁 *Melanie Bluelake's Dream* **by Betty Dorion**
At her new city school, Melanie misses her old friends on the Cree reserve, and she's angry with her mother for bringing her here. Most of all, she misses the loving warmth of her grandmother. Will she ever find a place she can truly call home? (a chapter book)

Up in the Sky

Look at the stars

Poem by Gerard Manley Hopkins

Look at the stars! look, look up at the skies!
O look at all the fire-folk sitting in the air!

Skywriting

Poem by
Marilyn Singer

Picture by
Kim Lafave

I want to be a pilot
   writing messages in the sky
Mysterious white words
   stretched wide between the clouds
that disappear in moments
   like letters printed in invisible ink
I want to make the man with the jackhammer
          the kid with the balloon
          the gardener
          the sunbather
          the first baseman
          the cop
All stop what they're doing
   look up at the same time
   and smile at this magic in the air
Then later wonder
   if it really was there

Personal Response

According to the poet, what is magical about skywriting? Do you agree with her feelings?

Imagine!

Invisible ink — now there's an idea! Invent a game based on disappearing messages.

Flying Billboards

Advertisements in the sky take several forms such as skywriting, banners towed by planes, hot air balloons, and huge blimps.

- Why do you think companies like to display their messages in the sky?
- What kinds of events might advertisers choose as good places to attract people's attention?
- Do you think "flying billboards" are a good idea? Give reasons for your answer.

Be A Skywriter!

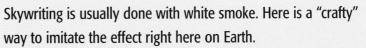

Skywriting is usually done with white smoke. Here is a "crafty" way to imitate the effect right here on Earth.

1. Make up a short message that you'd like to write in the sky.
2. Find or paint a large piece of sky-blue Bristol board for your background.
3. Use puffy white cotton batting to write your message. When it's ready, use a glue stick to attach it to the Bristol board.
4. Ask if you and your classmates can hang your messages from the ceiling.

Do you ever dream about flying? Think about what would be your favourite way to fly.

Balloon Ride

Story and Photographs by *Evelyn Clarke Mott*

E arly in the morning, Megan runs outside. The sky is blue and a gentle breeze blows against her face.

"Hooray!" she shouts. "It's a perfect day to ride in a hot air balloon."

Megan laughs with excitement as she races toward the launch field. The first person she meets is Joy, the pilot.

"Will you show me your balloon?" Megan asks.

"I'll be glad to," Joy replies. "Come with me. I'll show you how we get the balloon ready to fly."

Megan and Joy watch two women unroll the big balloon across the field.

"Elaine and Betty are my ground crew," Joy says. "First, they help get Firefly ready for flight. Then, when we're up in the air, Elaine and Betty follow us in the van to help us land."

"What's that on the ground?" Megan asks. "It looks like a long snake."

Joy laughs. "It looks funny, doesn't it? That's our balloon. We call it Firefly."

"Can I help, too, Joy?"

"Sure, Megan. This is the basket we will stand in. It's called a gondola. You can help me hook the cables to the balloon and gondola."

"Wow!" Megan exclaims. "There are a lot of cables."

"Yes." Joy smiles. "They keep the balloon and the gondola together."

Elaine and Joy hold open the mouth of the balloon, and Betty starts a large fan. WHIRRRRRRRR! The air blows into the balloon. Firefly begins to take shape.

"What are you doing?" Megan asks.

"We're filling the balloon with cold air."

"Cold air!" Megan exclaims. "But I thought Firefly was a hot air balloon."

"It is," Joy says. "After Firefly is filled with cold air, we heat the air with a flame.

"Before we do that, we must make sure the inside of the balloon is safe."

Megan and Joy walk inside Firefly and look it over carefully. Megan feels as if she is walking inside a big tent.

"The balloon is in good shape, no rips or tears," Joy says. "It's time to heat the air inside of it."

Joy lights the gas burner above the gondola.

"Hold your ears, Megan!" She opens the blast valve and shoots quick blasts of flame into the balloon. The burner sounds like a thousand roaring lions. RRRRROAR! RRRRROAR! RRRRROAR! RRRRROAR!

With each blast, the air inside the balloon gets warmer. Elaine and Betty hold Firefly down as it starts to rise.

"What makes Firefly fly?" Megan asks.

"Hot air," answers Joy. "Hot air weighs less than cold air. So, when the air in Firefly is heated, the balloon goes up into the sky."

Joy makes a last check of the instruments, the burners, the gas tanks, and the lines. She shouts, "All aboard!"

Joy helps Megan into the gondola and then turns the burner on for a long time. RRRRRRRRRROAR!

Firefly gently takes off into the open sky.

"Hooray!" Megan yells. "Here we go!"

Firefly starts out low... RRRRROAR! ...and then goes higher.

The balloon drifts across the sky. Megan sees treetops and fields, horses and farms, a skydiver, and Firefly's shadow. Megan and Joy smile when a bird flies underneath them.

Megan asks, "Where are we going?"

"Wherever the wind takes us," Joy answers. "Balloons can't be steered the way cars or airplanes can. I can only control how high or low we fly."

"But I don't feel any wind," Megan says.

"That's right," Joy says. "Since we're travelling with the wind, we don't feel the wind at all."

"Look, Megan. This is a compass. It tells us the direction we're travelling in. The wind is taking us to the north.

"The altimeter measures how high we are. Firefly is 1000 feet up."

Megan looks up into the balloon.

"It's so pretty," she says. "It looks like the quilt my grandma made me—only bigger!"

Joy turns off the burner and waits for the air inside the balloon to cool a little. Firefly starts to come down slowly.

"Let's go treetopping!" Joy lowers Firefly until its gondola scrapes the treetops.

Megan reaches out and grabs a fistful of leaves from a tall tree.

"This is fun!" she shouts.

Joy gets in touch with Elaine by radio. "Can you see Firefly?" she asks.

"Yes, Joy. We're right with you."

"Good," Joy says. "There's an open field ahead of me that would be a great place to land. Could you get the owner's permission?"

A few minutes later, Elaine radios Joy, "Permission granted." Joy opens the release vent. Hot air slowly escapes from the balloon. Firefly drifts lower and lower toward the ground. THUMP! BUMP! Firefly lands.

Joy tugs the rip cord. The top of the balloon opens up and Firefly sighs as the hot air rushes out.

"Yea!" Megan cheers as she steps from the gondola.

Joy presents Megan with a Certificate of Ballooning Excellence.

"Congratulations!" Joy says. "You did a great job." Megan smiles widely and gives Joy a hug.

"Would you help me pack up Firefly, Megan?"

Megan helps Joy stuff the long balloon into a cloth bag. Then, Elaine and Betty load the bag, basket, and burners into the van.

"Let's go home!" Joy says.

Clutching her certificate, Megan hops into the van. With her head in the clouds, she happily leans back for the ride home. ◗

FOLLOW UP

What are the best things about ballooning? What things about it could be scary?

Did You Know

The first successful flight people ever made was in a hot air balloon. The balloon was built by the Montgolfier brothers in France. On November 21, 1783, two passengers soared into the skies above Paris. Their historic flight lasted 25 minutes.

Understanding the Article

Pilot's Manual

Now that you have read the article closely, and examined the photographs, you've become an expert (almost) on flying balloons!

Work with a small group. Take the information in the article and turn it into a step-by-step instruction manual for new pilots. Begin by making notes about each step. Then decide how to number the steps. Be sure to include at least two **safety checks**. For fun, you might decide to illustrate each step.

TIP Use information from the photographs as well as the text.

When your group has finished, compare your instruction manual with the manuals other groups created.

YOUR TURN TO WRITE

A High-Flying Tale

When Megan looked down at the ground from the basket of the balloon, she saw things in a new way. We call this an "aerial view."

How would things look different from up in the sky? Imagine flying over the place where you live, or over an African plain full of animals, or above the North Pole during a dog-sled race. Are you flying on a magic carpet, in a rocket ship, or in a plane you designed yourself? Write a short story about your flight.

Imagine!

Make a BIG picture of your ideal balloon. Add it to a class mural!

The Science of Ballooning— Blowing Hot and Cold Air

It's a funny thing about air. You can't see it, and you can't feel it unless it's hot, cold, or windy. But without air, Megan could not have taken a balloon ride.

- Why does hot air make Firefly fly?
- How does Joy use the air to control the flight of the balloon?
- Why can't Megan feel the wind during her flight?
- What does Joy do to the air to make the balloon descend?

Experiment by Etta Kaner

Pictures by Dave Starrett

Get a Rise out of Air

Which is lighter, hot air or cold air? Try this experiment to help you find out, and you'll also discover how hot air balloons rise into the sky.

You'll need
- ✔ 2 large identical balloons
- ✔ scissors
- ✔ 2 straight pins
- ✔ 1 straw
- ✔ 1 piece of yarn 30 cm long
- ✔ 1 candle in a candleholder

1 Cut both balloons in half widthwise and discard the neck part.

2 Stick a pin into the centre of the rounded part of one balloon. Then stick the pin through the straw 1 cm from its end.

3 Attach the other balloon to the other end of the straw in the same way.

4 Pull the sides of the balloons apart so that they don't stick together.

5 Tie one end of the yarn near the middle of the straw. Tie the other end to a place where the straw can hang freely.

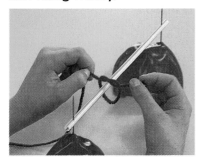

6 Move the yarn slowly along the straw until the two balloons balance.

7 Important: Do this part with an adult. Light the candle. Hold the candle about 12 cm underneath the opening of one balloon. What happens?

A Hot Air Balloon Record

People are always trying to set records. Balloonists are no different. In 1987, two men set a world record for crossing the Atlantic Ocean in a hot air balloon. They started out from Maine, U.S.A. and landed in Northern Ireland. The balloon used on this flight was as tall as a 21-storey building. Can you imagine the excitement in Ireland as people there watched a balloon the size of an apartment building descend from the sky?

How does it work?

The candle flame warmed the air inside the balloon. When air is heated, its molecules move farther apart. Since there is more space between the molecules, the hot air is lighter. The heated balloon rises because its air is lighter than the cooler air in the other balloon.

Hot air balloons use this principle to rise into the air. Attached to the bottom of the nylon balloon is a basket or gondola which carries a propane gas burner. The flame from this burner heats the air inside the balloon which is open at the bottom. To bring the balloon down, the air inside is allowed to cool.

Some balloonists fill their balloons with helium instead of hot air. Since this gas is much lighter than air, the basket or gondola attached to the balloon carries weights. The weights are usually bags filled with sand. By throwing sandbags overboard, the balloonist controls the height that the balloon rises. ◆

FOLLOW UP

Check your prediction. Which is lighter, hot air or cold? Do you think the experiment will be simple to do?

Try the experiment yourself!

Work with a group of friends.

Collect the materials. Follow steps 1 to 6. Ask an adult to help you with step 7.

Understanding the Article

Explaining the Experiment

- Did you follow the steps of the experiment in order? Why is this necessary?

- What happened when you held a candle under the opening of one balloon? Were you surprised?

- Why is hot air lighter than cold air? Which part of the article gave you the explanation?

- What is the difference between a hot air balloon and a helium balloon?

Did You Know ?

A molecule is a tiny, invisible particle. Everything around you, including air, is made up of molecules. A piece of paper is about 100 000 molecules thick!

Find Out About...

Hot air ballooning is a popular form of recreation. Use the Internet, the library, or a travel agent to find out where people go for balloon rides in your region. There are also ballooning festivals in Canada — a very colourful sight!

For a start, try the Web site for the Canadian Balloon Association http://gpu.srv.ualberta.ca/~anagorsk/cba.htm#events

Home Link

Cold Air Experiment

by Etta Kaner

Which takes up less space, warm air or cold air? Make a prediction, then try this balloon experiment at home.

You'll need
- a balloon
- a felt pen
- a measuring tape
- a refrigerator

1. Inflate the balloon and tie it tightly.

2. Measure the balloon around its widest part. Mark the balloon with a felt pen where you measured it.

3. Put the balloon in the freezer overnight.

4. In the morning, measure the chilled balloon around its widest part.

Is the balloon bigger when it's filled with warm air or with cold air?

What do you think happened to the air molecules inside the balloon when it was in the freezer?

How does it work?

Air is made up of tiny invisible particles called molecules. When air is cold, the molecules move closer together. That's why cold air takes up less space. When the cold air in the balloon contracted in the freezer, the balloon got smaller.

What would happen if

- ☛ you leave the balloon in the freezer longer?
- ☛ you hold the balloon under hot water for a few minutes?
- ☛ you fill the balloon with water and do the same experiment?

Discuss your predictions with a partner.

Big Number Quiz:

• How big is the Sun?

• How far away is
  the Sun?

• How old is the Sun?

Write your best
estimates in your
notebook.

The Sun: Earth's Star

Ancient people knew the Sun brought light and warmth. But they didn't know what made it shine and where it went each night. So they made up stories to help them understand the secrets of the Sun.

Article by
**Paulette
Bourgeois**

Illustrations
by
**Bill
Slavin**

Sun Tales

Long ago, the Egyptians thought the sky goddess, Nut, swallowed the Sun every night and gave birth to a new Sun the next morning.

People in Lithuania in eastern Europe told a different story. The Sun and Moon fell in love and got married. They had a baby and named her Earth. But the parents were always fighting. The Moon told the Sun to stop being so hot. The Sun told the Moon to stop being cold. They decided to separate.

But they both wanted to keep Earth. When they couldn't decide what to do, they visited the great god Thunder. Thunder told the Sun to take care of her daughter from morning until night and told the Moon to take care of Earth during the night.

And that's the way it's always been. Once in a while, when the Moon is too busy, his sisters, the stars, shine on Earth.

What is the Sun?

The Sun is a star—a bright, big ball of burning gas. It seems much larger than any other star because it is so much closer. The Sun is 150 million km away from Earth. That seems like a long way but if the Sun were closer, nothing on Earth could survive the heat.

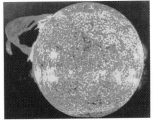

A loop of gas erupts from the Sun's surface.

Sun Facts

The Sun measures 1 392 000 km across. If the Sun was an empty ball you could fit one million Earths inside it.

The Sun weighs 2 billion billion billion t. That's 2 with 27 zeros after it. That's 333 000 times as much as Earth!

The Sun's gravity is 28 times greater than Earth's. If you weigh 45 kg on Earth, you'd weigh almost 1.5 t on the Sun!

The Sun is 4.5 billion years old.

How big a star is the Sun?

The Sun is a medium-sized star. Scientists say stars come in all sizes—anywhere from dwarf to giant size. They can be almost as small as Earth or 40 times as big as the Sun. Stars can glow blue (which means they are very hot), white, yellow, or red (much cooler). Scientists call our Sun a yellow dwarf.

What does the Sun do?

The Sun gives us light and heat. The Sun's light makes plants grow. Plants give us food to eat and oxygen to breathe. We would die without them.

The Sun's heat gives us rain. When the Sun warms lakes and oceans some of the water changes into a gas called water vapour. This gas floats high in the sky to where the air is cooler. The water vapour is chilled and changes back into water drops. When a lot of these drops join together, they form clouds. If the water drops get large enough, they fall as rain.

The Sun's heat also gives us wind. The heat warms the air and when air is warm, it moves. And wind is moving air.

If there was no Sun, Earth would have no wind, rain, heat, or light.

When did the Sun start to shine?

The Sun started to shine 4.5 billion years ago.

Long, long before that, there were nothing but gases floating around in the universe. About 12 billion years ago, pockets of gas gathered together to form the Milky Way galaxy. Over time, hundreds of billions of stars were born inside the Milky Way.

Our Sun was one of those stars. It started as an enormous cool cloud of gas and dust. It became smaller and hotter until it started to shine.

Will the Sun shine forever?

No, all stars die. In about 5 billion years the Sun will start to glow red and grow bigger. It will become so hot that the ice at Earth's North Pole will melt and the oceans will begin to boil. The Sun will continue to grow until it swallows the planets closest to it—including Earth! Then the Sun will begin to shrink and become dimmer and dimmer until it is a small, dim star called a white dwarf.

Sun Stuff

The solar system is the name given to the Sun and everything that travels around it, including the planets and their moons. Solar means "about the sun."

FOLLOW UP

How did you do on the Big Number Quiz? Compare your answers to the big numbers you read in the article.

Research — The Solar System

Make a big labelled diagram of the Solar System.
You'll need to know

* the names of all the planets

* how close or far from the Sun each planet is

* the shape of the orbit each planet makes around the Sun

* whether the planet has one or more moons circling around it

Choose one or two of the planets and find out more about them. Are they hot or cold? wet or dry? clear or cloudy?

Learn about how the planets got their names.
There is a Greek or Roman story about each of them.

Glossary

galaxy: a huge collection of stars, planets, dust, and gas

gas: a form of matter made up of tiny particles that can move freely in space

gravity: the invisible force that holds everything on Earth, and keeps Earth and planets circling around the Sun

matter: a solid, a liquid, or a gas

oxygen: a gas that makes up about 20% of the air on Earth

star: a ball of burning gas that gives off light

Understanding the Selection

Secrets of the Sun

* What is the name of the star that is closest to Earth?

* Why do living creatures on Earth need the Sun?

* What is the Solar System? How many planets can you name?

* Scientists believe the Sun is in the middle of its life span. Find evidence in the article to show why.

Look Safely at the Sun

A Sun Tale

Which Sun Tale in the article did you like the best? Why?

Make up your own tale to explain how the Sun and the Moon came to be up in the sky. Illustrate your tale and add it to a class anthology of Sun Tales.

You should never look directly at the Sun. But here is a safe way to see it.

You'll need
* a sunny day
* tape
* a large piece of white paper
* a small square of cardboard
* a small nail
* a stake or stick
* a bucket of sand
* a mirror
* an adult helper

1. Tape the paper to a wall outside.

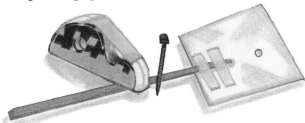

2. Have an adult punch a hole in the centre of the cardboard with the nail.
   Tape the stick to the cardboard, being careful not to cover the hole.

3. Stand the stick in the bucket of sand. Place the bucket in front of the paper on the wall.

4. Ask a friend to hold the mirror toward the sun, and move it until it reflects the Sun through the hole in the cardboard. Look at the white paper until you see an image of the Sun. Draw what you see.

Did you see any dark spots on the Sun? These are "sunspots."

Following Directions — Make sure you understand all the directions before you start.

Retell the steps in your own words to a partner.

BEFORE READING

Kataujaq, her family, and her people are Inuit. They live in Canada's Arctic. What do you know about the Inuit and the Arctic?

esker: a winding ridge of sand or gravel

taima: Inuit word meaning "that's all"

Northern Lights: The Soccer Trails

Story by
Michael Arvaarluk Kusugak
Pictures by
Vladyana Krykorka

1.

A LONG TIME AGO, when Kataujaq was little, her mother said, "We called you Kataujaq because, when you were born, you were as pretty as a rainbow." She put her nose to Kataujaq's, sniffed and said, "Mamaq," which means "You smell so nice." You see, that is the way we kiss. Some people call it rubbing noses but it is really sniffing. And Kataujaq hugged her mother by the neck, pressed her nose on her face and said, "Mamaq!" Kataujaq just loved her mother.

IN SPRING, the sun was still up in the sky when Kataujaq went to bed. When she woke up, early the next morning, it was already way up in the sky again. In spring, they would all go fishing.

They travelled on the sea ice. Kataujaq sat with her mother and her grandmother in the big canoe on the sled. It was very rough and there was a lot of water on the ice. The dogs' paws went "Slosh, slosh, slosh, slosh..." and the sled creaked. Kataujaq's father ran along beside it, holding onto the bow of the canoe, pushing this way, pulling that way, guiding the sled. "Hut, hut, hut," he said to the dogs, and they turned left.

Sometimes they had to go over big cracks in the ice. Kataujaq's father threw the dogs into the water and made them swim across. As they climbed out of the water, the dogs shook their fur, throwing tiny droplets of water everywhere which sparkled in the bright sunlight. Then Kataujaq's father made the dogs pull the sled across with the canoe and the people in it. Kataujaq and her mother screamed, "Aaiee!!" and hugged each other really hard because the water was dark and ominous looking. And sometimes they came upon seal holes where the water was flowing in, swirling like a whirlpool. Just the thought of them made Kataujaq shudder. She was glad she had her mother to hang on to.

When they got back on land they went to a lake called The Nose. It has a string of little islands in it that look like noses sticking up out of the ice. Kataujaq's mother caught a fish that was as big as Kataujaq.

IN SUMMER, Kataujaq loved to go for walks. One day, as she walked, Kataujaq picked a flower. It was a teeny tiny flower with delicate white petals. "My mom will like this," she said to herself. She collected many more beautiful tiny flowers. When she got home, she gave them to her mother. Her mother hugged her and kissed her and said, "They are beautiful. Thank you." She put them in a glass and kept them for a long time. She kept them even when they were dried up and did not look very nice anymore. Then Kataujaq went for another walk and collected more tiny flowers.

Sometimes she collected nice rocks: grey ones, white caribou-fat ones, flat ones, and smooth round ones. And her mother loved every one. She put them on the window sill. One day, Kataujaq's father tried to throw one away. Her mother said, "What are you doing? Put it back!" She was very stern about it and he put it back.

LATE SUMMER, just after the weather turns cool and the mosquitoes have gone, is the very best time to pick berries. The ground turns a fuzzy brown colour, it begins to get dark at night and the geese begin to form flocks, getting ready to fly away before winter comes. It was Kataujaq's *most* favourite time of year because she got to spend so much time outside with her mother. They picked berries on the long esker that lay just north of their house. Kataujaq's mother loved to pick berries. It took them a long time to fill a big can, but they did it. Kataujaq's face and hands turned purple with berry juice because she ate most of the berries she picked. Oh, what fun it was.

Sometimes they just played together. Kataujaq's mother would juggle stones and sing a juggling song:

> **Ai jaa ju ru jun nii**
> **A ja jaa ju ru jun nii**
> **Three for my cousin**
> **One for me**
> **Sounds like thunder**
> **Sounds like thunder**
> **Rainbow in the sky**
> **Rainbow in the sky**

Her mother taught Kataujaq all kinds of neat stuff that they had done when she herself was little. They had so much fun.

But that was a long time ago.

2.

ONE DAY, a big sickness came. So many people were sick. Kataujaq's mother coughed and coughed and they sent her away, way down south in an airplane. And she never came home again. Nobody told Kataujaq what had happened. She was too little. Her mother just never came home again.

It was such a long time ago. Now Kataujaq was a big girl; well, almost a big girl. But she still missed her mother a lot. These days she picked tiny flowers for her kindly grandmother, but it was not the same. When she picked berries on the long esker, just north of her house, she thought about her mother. When she picked up a nice rock, she thought about her mother. Sometimes, when she was alone, Kataujaq cried. Sometimes, when she went to bed at night and thoughts came, she cried a lot.

IN THE FALL, ice forms on the lakes and the sea. At night, when the sky is clear, you can see the stars, millions of them, twinkling through the moonlight. And sometimes you can see the droppings of the stars come streaking across the sky and disappear before they reach the horizon. Kataujaq loved to watch the sky and the stars. Sometimes she would wait a long time to see star droppings streak across the sky.

It was in early winter that the people in her village liked to go out and play soccer. They made a soccer ball out of caribou skin and stuffed it full of dry moss and fur. Then at night, in the moonlight, they went out on the sea ice, set up two goals made of ice blocks and played. Anybody who came down to the sea ice joined in the game. They would run for miles and miles, all night long. It was such fun.

SOMETIMES the northern lights came out.
They are thin strands of light, thousands of thin strands of light, that move about from here to there like thousands of people running around, following one another.

Kataujaq's grandmother liked to come out and watch the people play soccer too, and one night, when Kataujaq was feeling very sad and lonely, her grandmother told her a story.

"People die," she said. "And, when they die, their souls leave their bodies and go up into the heavens, and there they live. The thousands of people who have passed before us all live up there in the sky. When they were on Earth, they too liked to play soccer. And, even though they no longer live among us, they still like to play. So, on a clear moonlit night, they go out on the giant field up there and play soccer. You can see them, thousands of them, all running around chasing their soccer ball all over the sky."

KATAUJAQ watched the northern lights. The thousands of strands of light looked like they were all running around after each other chasing a soccer ball. Kataujaq's grandmother continued her story:

"But, unlike us, they are immortal now and nothing hurts them anymore, so they use a huge, frozen walrus head with big tusks for a soccer ball. When they give that walrus head a mighty kick, it flies across the sky, and they all chase it from one corner of the sky to the other. If you whistle they will come closer, and, if you keep whistling, they will come even closer. But beware, they may come too near. If they do, that walrus head might come swooping down and, 'Bonk!' knock your head off. When they come too close, rub your fingernails together so they make a clicking sound. That will make them go away."

Kataujaq whistled. The northern lights came closer. She whistled some more and they came closer and still closer. She thought she heard a cracking sound. Was it the sound of a mighty kick on a hard, frozen walrus head? And she thought she heard a "Whoosh!" as it came whizzing by. It was an eerie sound, like giant tusks slicing the air. It sounded awfully near. Quickly, she rubbed her fingernails together, making a clicking sound, and eventually the strange noises began to go farther away.

"Is my mother up there?" Kataujaq asked her grandmother.

"Of course she is," her grandmother replied. "When it is like this I, too, like to come out here. I come to see your grandfather. He was a kind man who loved to play soccer. He would have loved you. He always wanted a granddaughter. Now he is up there with all the other people who have passed away. Seeing him having a wonderful time makes me feel so much better."

Kataujaq watched the northern lights play their game for a long time. She thought she could see her mother running around with all of them up there. She seemed to be having a good time. As her mother turned to run, Kataujaq thought she saw her smile down. Kataujaq was glad her mother had not gone away at all. She was not so lonely anymore. It made her feel so much better.

SOMETIME, when the moon is out and the stars are twinkling brightly in the frosty air, you should go outside and take a look. Maybe you will see the northern lights way up in the sky. They really are the souls of people who have died and, like us, they like to go out and have a good time. They love to play soccer. And if you look closely, maybe you will see someone special whom you thought had gone away forever. That special person has not really gone away at all. It is the most wonderful thing. *Taima* ◈

FOLLOW UP

How did the author and the artist help you to experience the Arctic and its people?

Understanding the Selection

Up in the Sky

- How did this story make you feel? Did you think the ending was happy or sad?

- The story has two parts. In the first part, Kataujaq was a little girl. In the second, she was "almost" a big girl. What sad event happened in between?

- According to Kataujak's grandmother, what is the link between the northern lights and the "soccer trails"?

- How did Kataujaq's grandmother help Kataujaq to feel better about losing her mother?

Viewing the Illustrations

Which of the illustrations is your favourite? Why?

What did you learn from the pictures about

- traditional Inuit clothing?
- Inuit toys and games?
- the four seasons in the Arctic?

Create a Card

Kataujaq remembers many special things that she enjoyed doing with her mother. What do you like to do with your favourite person?

List some of them. Then make a card to send to that person. On the front, draw a picture of the two of you doing the things you enjoy together. Write a message inside that tells how much you care.

Did You Know ?

The northern lights are caused by a strange wind called the solar wind. Every second, tons of bits of the Sun are blown into space. Some of these particles get trapped in Earth's atmosphere, and are pulled toward the North Pole by Earth's magnetic field. As the particles descend, they light up gases in Earth's atmosphere. Then you see colourful, dancing bands of light in the northern night sky!

YOUR TURN TO WRITE

Similes

Writers often use the words "like" or "as" to compare two different things, such as strands of light, and people playing soccer. These comparisons (also called similes) appeal to the imagination.

There are several beautiful comparisons in this story. Find the other half of each of these similes and write them in your notebook:

"The thousands of strands of light looked **like** _____"
"A string of little islands that look **like** _____"
Kataujaq's mother said, "You were as pretty **as** _____"
"It was an eerie sound, **like** _____"

Now make up your own similes for bodies that shine in the sky: northern lights, the Sun, the Moon, the planets, the stars.

Author Michael Kusugak is Inuit himself. You can read all about him, and artist Vladyana Krykorka, on page 90.

MEET THE AUTHOR AND THE ARTIST

Michael Kusugak and Vladyana Krykorka

by Susan Petersiel Berg

Michael Arvaarluk Kusugak

"I always wanted to write a really special story, the kind of story that makes you feel comfortable at the beginning, makes you cry in the middle, and makes you feel good in the end," says Michael Kusugak. That's why he wrote *Northern Lights: The Soccer Trails,* based on the Inuit story of the Northern Lights.

Writing was always part of Michael's life. He was born on Cape Fullerton,

NWT. At the age of six, he went away to school. "I did a lot of reading and writing," he says. When he grew up and had four kids, Michael began telling them stories about their people, the Inuit.

Then Robert Munsch came to visit Michael in Rankin Inlet. The famous children's author stayed with the Kusugaks. "My boys would ask him to tell stories at dinner," Michael explained. "One night I told him one story that my grandmother told me, then another. Bob said, 'Why don't you write your stories down?'" The two ended up writing *A Promise Is a Promise* together. It was Michael's first published book.

Vladyana Krykorka

A Promise Is a Promise was a first for Vladyana Krykorka, too — her first picture book. She had worked as an art director, then as an artist for a textbook publisher. But after her daughter was born, Vladyana decided to work from her home.

"I sent my work to Annick Press, and they liked it," says Vladyana. "It was just good timing. The publishers had received Michael's book and were looking for an illustrator." Since then Vladyana has illustrated ten picture books, including six of Michael's.

Vladyana was born in Prague. "My mother was my first art teacher," she explains. "When I was 13, she signed me up for private classes." Vladyana went to a special art high school, then later studied illustration, design, and architecture. She came to Canada in 1968.

To research Michael's first book, Vladyana went to the library and watched a lot of videos on the North.

Then Michael asked her to illustrate his second book as well. "That's when I decided I needed to go to the Arctic myself," says Vladyana. Now she visits Rankin Inlet for each of Michael's books.

"I find Inuit culture really exciting!" she says. "I sketch and take photos. I do a lot of research so I can do the best possible job."

The "K" Team

How do two people work on a book together when they live so far apart? "A lot of faxes," they both laugh. Michael comes up with the story idea. When he's finished writing, he sends the story to his publisher, who sends it to Vladyana.

"First I do rough drawings," she says. Then she sends the roughs to Michael, who suggests changes. When both "K's" are agreed, Vladyana paints her final pictures in watercolour on French paper.

It's not only the pictures that can change. "Sometimes she gets me to change the words," says Michael. "We work on everything as a team," says Vladyana.

And, as Michael says at the end of *Northern Lights: The Soccer Trails,* "*Taima.* That's all." ◈

BEFORE READING

Have you seen the Big Dipper? Do you know the names of any other constellations? Make a class list before you read the article.

Starry Summer Night

Article by Diane Bailey and Drew McKibben

t's dark. It's late. The campfire's just about out. The ghost stories have left you nervous and excited. But, before you snuggle into your sleeping bag for the night look up at the sky. High above you in that star-speckled space are ferocious monsters, beautiful maidens, gods, heroes, and hunters. Can't see them? Don't worry, you just have to know where they're hiding.

Thousands of years ago, sky watchers sorted the star patterns they saw into shapes and figures, then made up stories about them. A summer night in Canada is the perfect time to see some of these very special patterns, or constellations (kon-stuh-LAY-shuns). Remember, stars rise and set just like the Sun. So if you have trouble finding the patterns early in the night, just wait a little and try again. And, don't forget to use the star chart (on page 97) to help you find your way.

Start at the Big Dipper

The best place to start your skywatch is at the **Big Dipper**. Maybe you've already seen it. It has seven very bright stars and looks like a pot with a long, bent handle. In the summer you can find it by facing north and looking to your left in the sky.

The Big Dipper forms the neck and part of the body of a bigger constellation called the **Great Bear**, or **Ursa Major**. According to Greek legend, the bear was causing trouble here on Earth, so Hercules, a very strong man, picked it up by the tail and swung it into the sky. The Greeks believed that anyone who angered the gods could be plucked from the Earth and dangled from the sky as punishment.

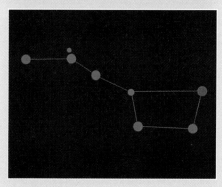

The Big Dipper

East to Little Bear

Not too far to the right of the Big Dipper is the **Little Dipper**. It is part of a constellation called **Little Bear**, or **Ursa Minor**. The Dippers look a lot alike, except that the Little Dipper is smaller. In the summer it looks like it's sitting upside down in the sky.

The last star in the Little Dipper's handle is very important. It's called **Polaris**, or the **North Star**, and if you learn to find it, you'll never get lost. Once you know which way is north, you can figure out all the other directions. Sailors long ago would use Polaris to help them find their way home again.

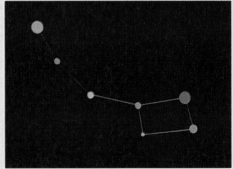

The Little Dipper

Queen of the Heavens

There's a queen in the sky and her name is **Cassiopeia** (kas-ee-oh-pee-ah). To find her, look to the right of Polaris at a cluster of five stars in the shape of a squished W resting on its side. It can also resemble an M or the number 3, depending on how you look at it.

That's the queen, although some people think that the W is just her throne. Cassiopeia thought she was the loveliest woman on Earth and boasted about her great beauty. The gods didn't like that and banished her to the sky, chaining her to her throne. At different times of the year, as extra

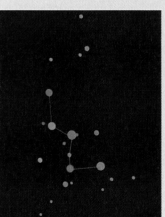

punishment, she hangs upside down in the sky. Now that's not very queenlike.

The constellation Cassiopeia

The Cross in the Summer Triangle

High overhead in the summer sky is a bright triangle of stars. It's one of the easiest patterns to see. To find it, run an imaginary line from the top star in the Cassiopeia W all the way up to the first bright star you see. That star is called **Deneb**. To the left of Deneb, and a little higher in the sky, is the star called **Vega**. These two stars form the base of the summer triangle. The point of the triangle is a star called **Altair**.

Each of the stars in the triangle is the brightest star in its own constellation. Deneb is at the head of a constellation called the **Northern Cross**. Some people call this constellation **Cygnus** (SIG-nus) the swan, and Deneb would be the end of its tail.

Altair is the eye of the constellation called **Aquila** (A-quill-ah), the eagle who carried the thunderbolts for Zeus, the king of the gods. The third star in the triangle, Vega, was called the vulture star by people in India and the Middle East.

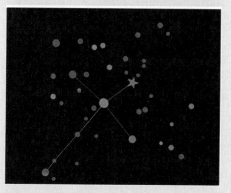

The constellation Cygnus, the Swan

The Northern Crown

To the left of Vega there's a small but beautiful crown called the **Corona Borealis** (bow-ree-AL-is). This group of six stars sits in the sky in the shape of the letter C. The Greek legend for this constellation claims that the god Dionysus (DAI-eh-NAI-sis) threw his crown up into the sky to prove his powers to a beautiful maiden called Ariadne (ar-ee-AD-nee).

The Shawnee First Nation didn't see the Corona Borealis as a crown. They believed it was a circle of star-maidens that danced in the sky. When one dancer came down to Earth, the circle was broken and the C shape was left.

The Herdsman

By looking to the left of the Corona Borealis you'll see a very bright star called **Arcturus**. This is the brightest star in **Bootes** (boh-OH-teez), a constellation that looks kind of like a squashed kite. In fact, to the Greeks, this grouping of stars looked like a plough. They thought that Bootes, the Herdsman, invented the plough, so they named this constellation after him.

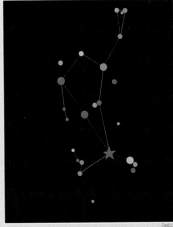

The constellation Bootes

Look Up in the Sky

Finding the constellations takes practice, especially because most of them don't really look much like the person or thing they were named for. To recognize the constellations, study the shapes of two or three of them in the **star chart.** Then go out at night and find them.

Once you've learned to spot the constellations, try playing your own game of connect-the-dots. Let your imagination run wild. You might be surprised at the pictures you can draw, and the stories you can tell, with the sky as your inspiration.

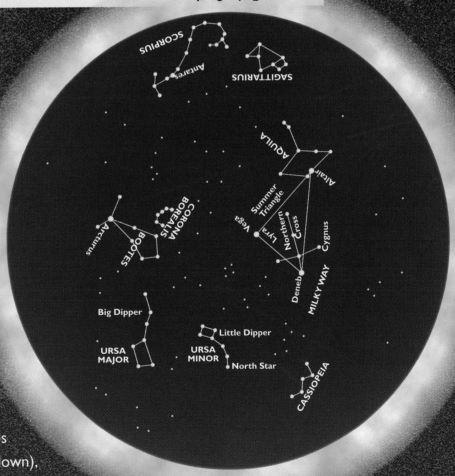

Facing South

SCORPIUS

Antares

SAGITTARIUS

AQUILA

Altair

Summer Triangle

Vega

Lyra

Northern Cross

Cygnus

Deneb

MILKY WAY

Arcturus

CORONA BOREALIS

BOOTES

Big Dipper

Little Dipper

URSA MAJOR

URSA MINOR

North Star

CASSIOPEIA

Facing North

Using the Star Chart

To find constellations, look north and hold this page overhead (facing down), or look south and turn the map upside down.

Complete your list of constellations with the new names in the article.

Understanding the Article

Matching Game

Match the names in the left column with the descriptions in the right column. Write the correct number and letter together in your notebook.

1. Big Dipper	a) a broken circle of dancing maidens
2. Cassiopeia	b) a big bear tossed by Hercules into the sky
3. Cygnus	c) in summer, it looks like an upside-down pot
4. Little Dipper	d) a swan-shaped constellation
5. Ursa Major	e) a queen who was too proud of her beauty
6. Corona Borealis	f) an eagle-shaped constellation
7. Polaris	g) seven bright stars in the shape of a pot
8. Little Bear	h) a constellation also called Ursa Minor
9. Aquila	i) the star that tells you which way is North

Congratulations! You're a star reader!

YOUR TURN TO WRITE

A Star Myth

Cultures around the world have different stories (or myths) to explain the same constellations. How did the ancient Greeks and the Shawnee First Nation explain the "Corona Borealis"?

Try writing your own myth to explain this or any other constellation. When you are finished, you might illustrate your myth. Then share it with a group of four or five classmates.

TIP When you've written your first draft, read it aloud to yourself or a partner. This will help you decide what revisions to make.

The Big Dipper

The North Star

North Star

Pointer Stars

The Big Dipper has many names around the world. The Vikings called it a wagon because it travelled around the sky. In China, it was a chariot that carried the king of the sky. The English still see it as a farmer's plough, while the Hindus of India say the Dipper's seven bright stars are seven wise men.

Looking at Language

PROPER NOUNS

The names of the constellations begin with capital letters (Great Bear, Bootes). That's because they are **proper nouns.** Proper nouns are the names of particular people (Julia, Dr. Wong, Canadians), places (Kenya, Mt. Everest), or things like dates, events, companies, and book titles (February, the Olympics, McDonald's, *The Wizard of Oz*).

Decide which of the nouns in the following paragraph should start with a capital letter. Write them in your notebook.

Add capital letters

A hundred years ago, slaves in the southern united states called the big dipper the drinking gourd. They knew that the two stars at the front of the bowl always point to the north star. So they used the drinking gourd as a compass to escape to the north. Barbara smucker 's novel, underground to canada, tells about their hair-raising journey.

Dear Earth

Poem by
Karla Kuskin

Picture by
Robert Johannsen

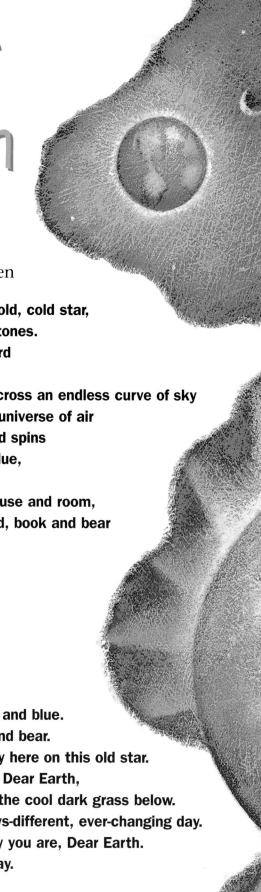

I'm sitting on an old, cold star,
me and a lot of stones.
Not a tree or a bird
or a chair.
I'm looking out across an endless curve of sky
across an empty universe of air
to where my world spins
tree green, sea blue,
there.
City, windows, house and room,
crayons, bike, bed, book and bear
there.
Snug
and VERY
far
far
far
away.
Dear Earth
I miss your green and blue.
I miss my room and bear.
It's dull and lonely here on this old star.
I miss your night, Dear Earth,
the moon above, the cool dark grass below.
I miss each always-different, ever-changing day.
You know the way you are, Dear Earth.
Well, stay that way.

Solve the puzzle!

Who is the speaker in the poem? How did he or she end up sitting on an old, cold star?

A Letter from Space

Imagine that you are an astronaut looking out the window of your space shuttle. You have been on your space mission for ten months now. As Earth comes into view far below, you decide to e-mail a letter home. Who will you write to? How are you feeling? What do you want to do the most when you get back? Write the letter!

MORE GOOD READING

Up in the Sky

Our Solar System
by Seymour Simon
This book takes you on a tour of our Solar System. You'll love the big, beautiful photographs of the sun, the moon, all nine planets, and more. See fiery Venus, mysterious Mars, ringed Saturn, and distant Pluto in colourful close-up detail. (a science book)

🍁 ***Balloon Science***
by Etta Kaner
Blow up some balloons and have a blast with this book! It's bursting with experiments and activities to show you how things work. Use ordinary balloons to discover how air holds up airplanes, build your own hovercraft, launch your own balloon rocket! (a science activity book)

🍁 ***Flight of the Space Quester***
by John Bianchi
Another crazy adventure with the Bungalo Boys! After careful preparations, the "astronauts" board the Space Quester at Funland. Are they blasting off into space? Or simply testing gravity on the roller coaster? Oops! Coming up fast: The Unknown Black Hole! (a cartoon book)

🍁 ***The Sun and The Moon***
by Paulette Bourgeois
Why does the Sun shine? How big is the Moon? These two books are filled with facts, photos, experiments, legends, and myths on the Sun and the Moon. They'll help you learn by reading and doing. (science books)

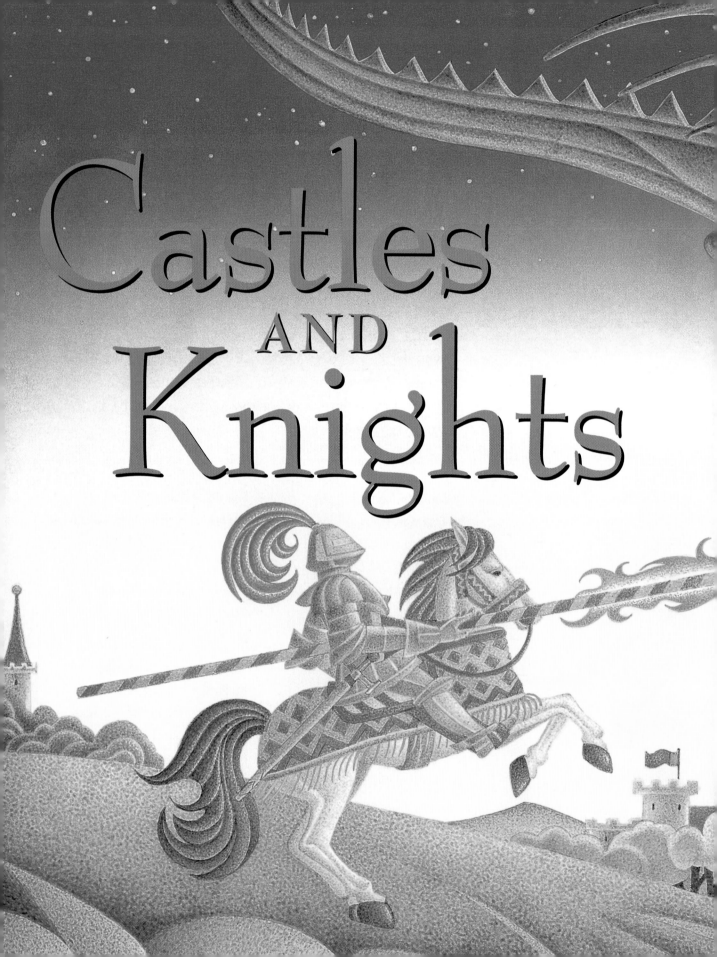

Castles
AND
Knights

Dragonbrag

Poem by Jack Prelutsky

Once upon a happenstance
I met a knight in armour.
I fixed my flame upon his lance —
It was a four-alarmer!

Castle
◆ LIFE ◆

Castles and Keeps by Christopher Maynard

During the Middle Ages, many rich and powerful lords lived in mighty castles. A castle protected its owner from bands of thieves, rival lords, and invaders from other lands.

The slowest way to capture a castle

An ironclad wooden portcullis was lowered over the door for extra security.

Soldiers could shoot out from slits in the walls.

High towers, called turrets, gave a good view of the enemy's forces.

In safekeeping

Early stone castles often consisted of just one tower, called a keep. They had incredibly thick walls and might be 35 m high. Prisoners kept in the keep very rarely escaped!

Fighting to the top

If the main door was built on the second floor, attackers had to force their way up a flight of steps before they could try to break in.

was to starve out the people inside.

The castle gate was guarded by strong towers, a wooden drawbridge, and a portcullis.

The moat kept attackers from digging under the main walls.

Charging with a lance
In jousts, knights fight one-on-one on horseback, knocking each other to the ground with lances. To practise, I aim my lance at a tilting post.

If I don't ride by quickly enough, the swinging weight will knock me off my horse.

Growing up in a Spanish Castle

by Chris & Melanie Rice

It is 1450 and Sancho is learning the skills of war. Already he can saddle a horse, wield a sword, and throw a javelin. He lives with his uncle, Don Pedro, who is a fierce warrior. Sancho hopes that one day he, too, will become a "caballero," or knight, and ride into battle.

The Castle
Sancho lives in a castle high on a hill. The castle is surrounded by thick stone walls.

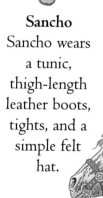

Sancho
Sancho wears a tunic, thigh-length leather boots, tights, and a simple felt hat.

Steel footwear

Steel helmet

Armour
When fully armed, Don Pedro is completely covered in plate armour, from the steel footwear on his feet to the helmet on his head.

Wooden lance

Shield

Helping Don Pedro
Sancho chooses the right saddle and bridle for Don Pedro's horse and then helps Don Pedro put on his armour. He knows how all the parts of a suit of armour fit together.

Mealtimes

Dinner plate

At mealtimes, Sancho is expected to carve the meat at the table, serve Don Pedro with his wine cup and dinner plate, and watch his manners!

Serving food

Sancho serves the food with broad-bladed knives like these.

Broad blades

Learning
Fighting is only one part of a knight's training. I am also taught to read, write, and count by the castle priest.

Entertainment

While the knights eat, visiting entertainers, called "minstrels" sing, play music, and tell stories.

Minstrels

Music

Music forms an important part of castle entertainment. Sancho is learning to play the lute. This modern lute is similar to the one he would have played.

Carved figure

Wooden saddles,

decorated with carvings, used for special occasions, such as parades.

Lute

Bedtime
I sleep on a bed of straw in the great hall with the other boys. At dawn we get up for mass.

The Inside Story

by Philip Steele

In early castles, life was far from comfortable. The wind whistled through wooden shutters in the windows, and most people slept on benches or on rough mattresses in the great hall. By the 1200s, castles had well-furnished bed chambers and living rooms heated by large open fires and lit by candles. The better rooms had glass windows and plastered walls hung with fine tapestries. Floors were covered with sweet-smelling herbs or rush matting.

1 The wardrobe
The top room in the lord's tower was used by the lady's personal servants. Linen and clothes were stored in large chests.

2 Master bedroom
This had rush mats on the floor and richly decorated walls. A lady-in-waiting could sleep on the trundle bed, which was pulled out from under the main bed.

3 The solar
This was the lord's private living room. After a hearty meal he might retire here for a game of chess.

4 Basement
A trapdoor from the solar led down to the basement. Weapons, coins, and other valuables might have been kept here.

Reading and writing

Few people in the Middle Ages knew how to read and write. There were not many schools, and most children never went to one. Boys had more opportunity to learn than girls, but there were still some famous women writers, such as Christine de Pisan, who lived in France in the 1400s.

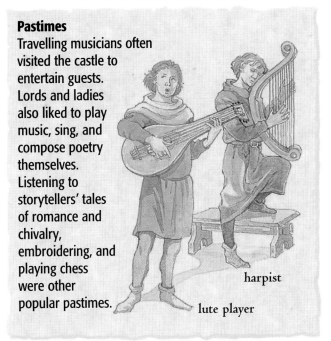

Pastimes

Travelling musicians often visited the castle to entertain guests. Lords and ladies also liked to play music, sing, and compose poetry themselves. Listening to storytellers' tales of romance and chivalry, embroidering, and playing chess were other popular pastimes.

harpist

lute player

The lady, the wife of the lord, usually played an important part in running the castle. She organized the servants and entertained visiting noblewomen. When the lord was away, she might inspect local farms or manage supplies and repairs to the castle. Even so, this was still a man's world. It was believed that women were inferior to men. In some places, they could not own land or make a will. ◆

Growing up

From the age of six or seven, the children of nobles were often sent to live in another lord's castle. Boys became pages and learned how to fight. Girls learned how to manage a household.

Marrying young

Marriages between nobles were arranged when the children were still in their cradles. Most lords and ladies were married by the time they were fourteen.

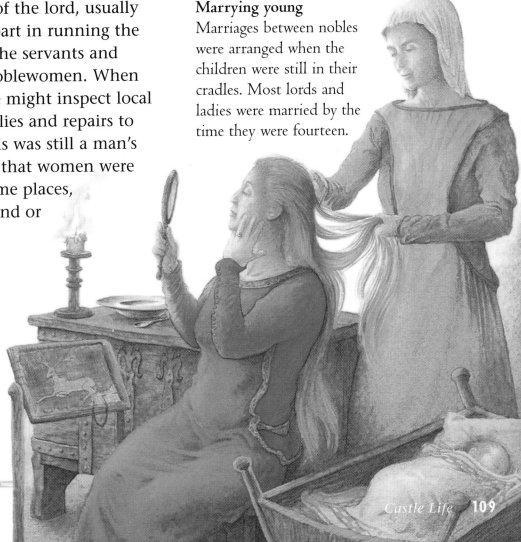

FOLLOW UP

Make a list of three new things you learned. Make another list of three questions you would still like to ask about castles, knights, or life in the Middle Ages.

Understanding the Article

Keeping Up to Castles

Castles and Keeps

- How do you think each of these castle parts helped the people inside to defend themselves?

turrets	the moat
slits in the walls	the staircase
the portcullis	the drawbridge

Growing Up in a Spanish Castle

- What was Sancho's goal in life?

- Sancho helped Don Pedro in many ways. Which of his jobs do you think would be the most interesting? Which would be the most difficult?

- Why do you think a young knight had to learn the following things?

jousting	playing the lute
putting on armour	reading, writing, and counting

The Inside Story

- Why were early castles uncomfortable? What improvements were made later?

- What important jobs did the lady of the castle do?

- How do you think the children of the castle felt when they turned six or seven?

- Why do you think marriages were arranged in the Middle Ages? Would you like your parents to select your marriage partner? Why, or why not?

Imagine!

You are a lady or a knight. You need a banner to fly from the castle tower. What colours will you choose? What symbols will you use?

Wooden shingles

Pagoda-like roof

Wooden upper story

Narrow window openings

Gun loop

Did You Know ?

There are castles in Canada! Casa Loma in Toronto was built in 1911 by a rich businessman named Sir Henry Pellatt. It has 98 rooms, 21 marble fireplaces, and 30 bathrooms! It even has two secret passages. It adds a flavour of the Middle Ages to a big, modern city.

Castles Around the World

One thousand years ago, noble lords built castles all over Europe and the Middle East. About 400 years ago, nobles in Japan also built many castles. This picture shows Himeji Castle (1609). It provided a home and protection for Japanese knights, who were called samurai.

Find Out More About...

- how Japanese castles were built
- the lives of the samurai and their families

Use the library and the Internet. Present your information as a display of pictures with captions.

Why do kings and queens need an heir? Who is the present heir to the British throne?

THE Sword in the Stone

Story by
Angela Wilkes

Pictures by
Peter Dennis

*L*ONG, LONG AGO, in Britain, when the world was still full of magic, there was a wise old wizard called Merlin. He could see into the future and work magic spells.

One wild and stormy winter's night Merlin was staying in a castle. It was the stronghold of his friend, King Uther. The queen had just given birth to Uther's first and only son.

The king told Merlin he feared a plot to kill his son and that he had a plan to keep him safe.

Just before midnight, Merlin opened a small, secret door and slipped out of the castle. Under his cloak he was carrying a bundle, and in the bundle was the baby boy.

2

3

4

The years passed and Uther died. No one knew he had a son to inherit his crown, so his knights fought each other to win the kingdom.

Far away in the Welsh hills, Merlin heard of these fights for the crown. As only he knew that Uther had a son, he set off at once for London.

There Merlin said to the archbishop, "The time has come to find the new king. You must call all the knights in the land to London."

5

The archbishop summoned all the knights to come on Christmas Day. Hundreds came and they crowded into the Abbey to pray. After the service, as they were leaving, they stopped in amazement.

A huge block of stone had appeared in the churchyard and in it was a sword. Round the stone were carved the words: WHOEVER PULLS THIS SWORD OUT OF THIS STONE IS THE TRUE BORN KING OF BRITAIN.

6

Eagerly the knights leapt on to the stone and one after another they struggled to pull out the sword. Even the strongest knights could not move it an inch. "The king is not here," said the archbishop.

7

"Send messengers round the kingdom," he ordered. "Tell every knight what is written on the stone. On New Year's Day we shall hold a tournament. Perhaps the king will be amongst those who come to joust."

8

Knights, with their squires, families, and servants, rode to London from all over the land. They set up their tents on the field and practised for the tournament.

On New Year's Day the knights went to the Abbey churchyard. Each one tried to pull the sword out of the stone, but struggle as they might, no one could move it.

9

Among the knights who came to London for the tournament were Sir Ector and his two sons, Kay and Arthur. Kay had just been knighted but Arthur was only sixteen and was too young to be a knight.

10

On the way to the tournament Sir Kay suddenly found he had forgotten his sword. "I must have left it at the inn," he said. "I will fetch it for you," said Arthur and set off at a gallop for the town.

11

When he reached the inn, the door was locked. Arthur knocked but everyone had gone to the tournament. "I must find a sword," he thought. "This is Kay's first joust and he cannot fight without one."

12

He rode away, wondering what to do. Passing the Abbey churchyard, he saw the sword in the stone. Without reading the words on the stone, he leapt off his horse, ran to the stone and pulled out the sword.

The Sword in the Stone **115**

13

Arthur galloped back to the tournament. "Here's a sword," he said, handing it to Kay. Kay stared at it for a moment, then looked at Arthur. He knew where the sword came from and snatched it.

14

He hurried to Sir Ector. "Look, father," he shouted. "Here is the sword from the stone. I must be the King of Britain." But Sir Ector knew his son well. "Let us go back to the churchyard," he said quietly.

15

In the Abbey, Sir Ector made his elder son swear on the Bible to tell the truth about the sword. Kay bowed his head and said, "Arthur gave it to me." Then Arthur told Sir Ector what he had done.

16

They went into the churchyard and Arthur put the sword back into the stone. Sir Ector seized it but it would not move. Then Kay tried but it still would not move. "It is your turn, Arthur," said Sir Ector.

17

18

Arthur gripped the sword, pulled and it slid easily out of the stone. Sir Ector and Kay knelt down at once. Arthur looked at them in surprise. "What is the matter? Why are you kneeling?" he asked.

"Read the words on the stone," said Sir Ector. "I am not your real father," he explained. "When you were a baby, Merlin brought you to me so that you would be safe from Uther's enemies.

19

"Now we must tell the archbishop that we have found the king." But the other knights would not believe it. They went back to their homes, agreeing to meet again in London to settle the matter. They met at Whitsun and crowds

watched the knights try their luck. Only Arthur could pull out the sword. The crowds shouted, "Arthur is king!" And knights and people knelt to swear their loyalty. ◈

FOLLOW UP

In the story, the true heir to the throne could not be found. How did the sword in the stone solve this problem?

Understanding the Story

In Days of Magic

- Why did King Uther ask Merlin to take his son away?
- What trouble happened in Britain after King Uther died?
- Who do you think put a magic spell on the sword in the stone?
- What did Kay do that showed he should not be king?
- Do you predict that Arthur will make a good king or a bad king? Give reasons for your answer.

Imagine!

You are Arthur, and you have become king at the age of 16. Write a letter to Merlin, telling him your plans and asking for advice.

Story Structure

Complete this chart in your notebook.

The Sword in the Stone

Characters

1. _____ a wizard
2. _____ King of Britain
3. _____ a knight
4. _____ the knight's son
5. _____ the knight's adopted son

Setting

1. _____ place where the story happened
2. _____ time when the story happened

Problem to be Solved

_____
_____

Media Link

The Legend of King Arthur

The legends say that Arthur went on to become a great king. He married Queen Guinevere, and they lived in a castle called Camelot. He and his "Knights of the Round Table" vowed to be true to the code of chivalry. They had wonderful adventures, too. See page 143 to help you find more stories about King Arthur.

The musical movie, *Camelot,* is based on the stories of King Arthur and his knights. The science fiction movie, *Star Wars,* is about "knights" of the future, whose adventures take place in space. When you watch it, compare the movie characters with the characters in *The Sword in the Stone.* Who has magic powers like Merlin? Who carries a shining sword? Who is the enemy? Who is the young hero?

Knights are supposed to be strong and brave, and to protect the lord and his people. Read on to see how the knights behave in this story!

Story and
Pictures by
*Donald
Carrick*

HARALD
AND THE
GIANT KNIGHT

Harald lived with his mother, Helga, and his father, Walter, in the valley which spread beneath the castle.

The valley was owned by a baron who lived in the castle, surrounded by his knights. All the farmers in the valley had to give the baron part of their crops.

He, in turn, allowed them to farm his land. Harald's family had farmed the same land for as long as anyone could remember.

Harald's father was a weaver as well as a farmer. He wove eel traps, screens, hats, fences, chairs, and every manner of basket.

One spring morning Harald climbed up to the castle with baskets his father had woven for the castle kitchen. Harald went to the castle as often as he could.

After he delivered the baskets, he wandered through the passageways, exploring the wondrous stone chambers. Many were larger than his home.

Harald was especially fond of the baron's knights. Knights were different from other folk. They were huge, scarred men who wore leather and metal clothes covered by bright tunics. The knights spoke with deep voices and their clothing creaked and clanked as they walked by. Harald burned to be one of them.

Harald loved the jousts when two knights fought. Best of all were the tournaments. Then he could watch all the baron's knights clash with all the knights from another castle in a mock battle. Nothing made Harald happier than to see the galloping horses and the swirling banners, and to hear the clang of sword against shield.

On this particular morning the Baron announced that it was time to begin training for the summer tournaments. A great cheer went up from the knights. They were restless after the long winter they had spent inside the castle.

As Harald walked home, he wished he could train with them.

The next morning, a terrible racket woke Harald. He ran outside to find his father in a fit. Men from the castle were swarming all over their farm. Horns blew. Kettledrums boomed. Tents were going up.

"What's happening?" Harald asked.

"The knights regular practice fields are flooded, so they've come here to train," his father said. Harald watched as knights strutted about, shouting a thousand orders.

"We are ruined," groaned Walter. "With all this foolish practice on our fields, how can we plant the spring crops?"

Harald understood how his father felt. Without a harvest, his family would have no food and could not pay the baron for the use of his land. But at the same time, it was Harald's dream come true. All the knights were right here on his family's farm.

Walter's fields were transformed into a jousting arena in which the knights galloped about on large horses and practised with their lances.

Since no farming could be done, Harald spent all his time at the knights' camp. Soon he was helping with the horses and tending the fires. Perhaps there was a chance for him to become a knight after all.

The knights' presence changed everything on the farm. There were no more eggs to collect because the constant noise caused the chickens to stop laying. The pigs grew nervous and lost weight.

Harald could not believe it when knights tested their swords by chopping into his father's carefully tended fruit trees. The stone boundary fences his grandfather had built were broken and scattered.

The knights had huge appetites. To fill the camp cookpots they simply took what they wanted from Walter and the other valley farmers. Chickens, ducks, pigs, and goats disappeared in their stewpots and on the roasting spits.

Harald was shocked. He had always thought knights were strong, brave men who spent their time helping people. Instead, he saw them ruin the land and plunder the farms like thieves.

Walter was pleased when Harald announced one day that he was no longer going to the camp. Harald had lost his taste for the knightly life.

To save what little food they had left, Helga gathered it together and put it in a sack. When it was dark, Harald went with his father to hide it. They carried the food down a small path past the knights' camp to a secret cave. Harald had discovered the cave one day last summer while he was picking berries. They hid the food on a high ledge.

When they returned home, no one could sleep so they sat together around their small fire. There seemed to be no answer to their problem.

"If I were big, I'd thrash all the knights and send them running," said Harald. "It's the only thing they understand."

"No one is big enough to do that," answered Helga, "except another knight."

Walter said nothing, but his hands began weaving. The giant shadows his father cast on the wall gave Harald an idea.

"I know how we can get rid of the knights!" he said.

His father stopped weaving. "What do you mean, son?" he asked.

"Well, why can't we make a knight to frighten them?"

"And just how would we do that, Harald?" asked Helga.

"Father is a master weaver, isn't he? He can weave anything. Why can't he weave a giant knight?"

A smile spread over Walter's face. "Let's hear more," he said.

Excitedly they talked late into the night as idea led to idea. By morning they had a plan.

From the next day on, Harald's family spent all their time at the cave weaving their giant. Harald made trip after trip to the cave, bringing Walter great bundles of reeds.
One afternoon rabbit hunters from the camp almost discovered the cave as Harald was about to enter.

"Where are you bound with that bundle, lad?" called the leader, coming closer.

Harald knew that once the dogs got near the entrance to the cave, all would be lost. "Oh, I'm on my way to build a rabbit hutch," he replied, thinking quickly.

"Rabbits! What rabbits?" demanded the hunters.

"The rabbits in the thicket down the ravine. It's full of them," said Harald.

"Well lad, we'll just take a look at this thicket of yours," said the leader, and the hunters marched off.

With each bundle of Harald's reeds, the basket knight grew larger. Harald was very proud of his father's skill. He was sure nothing this large had ever been woven.

"By daylight, he will probably look rather patchy," Walter said. "But by night, after the knights have finished drinking and are asleep, our knight should be very frightening."

Helga decided to make a cape for him.

Finally the giant basket knight was finished. He was almost too large to squeeze through the cave entrance. Carefully they mounted the creature on Patience, their old plow horse, and tied it down.

Walter led Patience down the narrow trail. The knight looked huge but weighed so little that each draft from the valley caught it like a sail. Harald clung to a rope to steady the creature.

At one spot the trees were so close they almost pushed the basket giant off Patience's back. When the knight swayed back and forth it looked even more ghostlike.

"These paths were not made for giants," Harald whispered.

Each small farm along the way had a dog that barked as the giant drew near. Harald started to shiver. What if they were discovered? Fortunately no one woke.

When they arrived at the edge of camp, the knights were all asleep.

It was Harald's task to enter the camp and untie the horses. He slipped quietly past the tents full of snoring knights. By day he knew the camp, but by night it all seemed different. One mistake could ruin everything.

At last he found the horses and with trembling hands untied the knots. The freed horses began to wander through the camp.

In the light of the early moon, Harald saw the giant loom above the trees.

The moment he appeared, Walter and Helga began a horrific clamour. She clanged pots while he made loud, moaning sounds through a long wooden tube. That was the signal for Harald to dart from tent to tent, pulling up tent pegs. One after another, the tents collapsed on the sleeping knights.

The bewildered knights awoke in the dark, blanketed by the heavy tents. As they groped free, they tripped over ropes and cracked their shins on tent poles. Once they were in the open, the mob of bruised, half-clothed knights was startled by the sight of the giant. It seemed to be walking over the trees. And it began to shout at them in a deep, creaky voice.

"AWAY WITH YOU. AWAY FROM THE GRAVES OF MY FOREFATHERS. BEGONE, ALL OF YOU, BEFORE THE NEW DAY DAWNS!"

Then, suddenly, the swaying knight seemed to disappear from the sky. The frightened knights were left standing in the shambles of the camp. Actually, the giant had fallen from Patience's back and she trotted away, dragging him behind.

Harald caught up with his parents who were close on Patience's heels. They were busy picking up the bits and pieces that were falling from the giant. There was no time to wonder if their plan had worked until they reached the cave.

Dumbfounded, the knights milled about the camp gathering their wits and their horses. No trace of the ghostly giant could be found.

No one wanted to mention the ghost's warning, but one knight had the courage to say, "This camp is a wreck. I think it's time to leave."

"Let's go back to the castle," said a second.

A great sigh of relief came from all sides. Not one knight wanted to stay on and risk seeing the giant again.

Shortly after sunrise Harald, Helga, and Walter watched the band of knights make their way slowly up the hill toward the castle. Helga and Walter hugged each other and cried with relief. Harald, who could not contain himself, jumped for joy.

After a great deal of work, the three of them cleared their fields and planted crops. That fall their harvest was not as big as usual, but it was enough to pay the baron and feed themselves through the winter.

The next spring Harald and his father were planting once again.

"Listen to what the wind brings us from down the valley," said Walter. They could hear a faint clanging from the knights at practice on the baron's field. This time they were but pleasant tinkles to Harald's ears.

Nearby stood a familiar figure. It was a scarecrow, fashioned from the giant's reeds. As it turned with the wind, it almost seemed to smile. 🔹

How did you feel about the way the knights behaved in this story? Do you think it could be a true picture of life in the Middle Ages?

Understanding the Story

- Why did the farmers have to give the baron part of their harvest?
- Why did Harald admire the knights at first?
- What happened to change Harald's mind about the knights?
- How did Harald help his family to solve the problem the knights created?
- At the end, the scarecrow made from the basket knight "almost seemed to smile." If it could talk, what do you think it would say?

Imagine!
You've been asked to organize an exciting but non-violent tournament at your school. What activities will you include?

YOUR TURN TO WRITE

A Story

In *Harald and the Giant Knight,* the author has reversed the roles of his characters. Knights are usually brave, kind, and helpful — but in this story they are thoughtless and cowardly. Giants in stories are usually mean and rough, but in this story the giant helps the hero.

Think of a story (such as a fairy tale) in which there are good and wicked characters. Reverse the usual roles, then write your own version of the story in your notebook. To help you get started, make a list like this one.

Story Title	Good Characters	Wicked Characters
1. Snow White and the Seven Dwarfs	Snow White the dwarfs the Prince	the stepmother the huntsman
2.		

Act It Out!

Try acting out the last scene (page 126-127), when the giant knight scares the real knights away. You'll need a group to act as knights, plus sheets to substitute for their tents. Another group can be the horses, tied to tables and desks. Harald, our hero, will untie the horses. Helga and Walter need pots and pans and a long tube. One or two students can play Patience the horse, who carries the giant knight. And of course, you'll have to build a giant knight! (Out of paper, perhaps?)

Media
SPOTLIGHT

Have you ever wondered how an animated film is made? Follow the process step by step as you read this article.

Animating Harald

Article by
Catherine Rondina

Pictures by
Steve Attoe

YOU'VE JUST FINISHED reading *Harald and the Giant Knight*. What a great story! Harald's bravery and quick thinking saved his family's farm. I guess you could call him a hero.

This got me thinking about other storybook heroes, like Hercules and Wonder Woman. Then I had a cool idea. Like those two heroes, Harald could star in his own cartoon show! But how do you take a story from print to TV screen?

I decided to take my idea to the experts at Nelvana, an animation company in downtown Toronto. I'll bet you've seen some of the cartoon shows Nelvana has made, such as *Stickin' Around, Care Bears, Inspector Gadget,* or *Babar.*

There, I was introduced to Patricia Burns. Her job as Production Vice President keeps her very busy. She looks after everything: finding interesting stories, hiring a director, and seeing that shows are finished on time.

Ms. Burns thought *Harald and the Giant Knight* would make an excellent cartoon show. Let's pretend that Nelvana decided to turn the story into a half-hour animated film. Ms. Burns explains how they would do it.

STEP #1

THE BOOK BECOMES...A SCRIPT

The first thing Nelvana does is contact the publisher and the author of the book. The company needs to get permission to use Donald Carrick's story and its characters.

Next, a **scriptwriter** turns the story into a script. A script looks like a play. It gives all the dialogue the actors will speak, and all the directions the animators will need.

STEP #2

THE SCRIPT BECOMES...A STORYBOARD

A **director** takes charge of the project. It is his job to see that things run smoothly during the making of the film. The director takes the script to the story department. Together, they brainstorm about how to transform Harald into an animated film.

Next, **storyboard artists** make rough drawings to show how Harald and the other characters might look. There are hundreds of decisions to make—what the giant's face will look like, what colour Harald's horse Patience will be, what his mother will wear. Soon the story idea becomes a storyboard. A storyboard looks like a comic strip. Each frame contains a drawing, the words the characters speak, and directions for the camera.

STEP #3

THE STORYBOARD GETS A SOUNDTRACK

It's time to give the characters their voices. The director hires good **actors** to play each character. They use lots of expression to read their lines. It can take up to four hours to record a single voice for a half-hour show.

Next, realistic sound effects are created, like the clanging noises the swords make during a joust. A **composer** writes music to suit Harald's adventures and the Middle Ages setting. Then a **sound technician** records the voices, the sound effects, and the music to make the soundtrack for the film.

STEP #4

THE ANIMATORS
GET THINGS MOVING

Now the **layout artists** take over. They do drawings that show where each character should be placed in a scene. (An example is the scene where Harald and his father are weaving the giant knight in the cave.)

These drawings are sent to the **background artist**. She draws background scenes such as the castle in the distance, the family farm, and the inside of the cave. It's also her job to set the mood of the film.

Next the storyboard, the layouts, and the background drawings are taken to the **animators**. These key artists are the ones who make the characters move.

It may take four or five pencil drawings just to show a knight waving his sword! The chief animator makes the first and last drawings. The "in-betweeners" make — you guessed it! — the drawings in between.

HARALD BECOMES
AN ANIMATED FILM...IN COLOUR!

It's time to add colour to the drawings of Harald and his pals. The **ink and paint artists** choose from two styles of painting. The classic style is to paint by hand onto celluloid film sheets. The newer way is to use a computer. This way, the painter scans the drawings into a computer and paints them with a **digital painter.** He follows a chart which tells him what colours to use and where to click them onto the drawing. It's almost like paint-by-numbers!

Once the painting has been completed, the drawings are videotaped. The video is sent to the editing department. The **editors** match the video and the soundtrack so that pictures, voices, sound effects, and music fit together perfectly. Finally the film is finished!

If the show is popular, it will be shown on television stations all over the world. If it's really popular, Harald and the giant knight will turn up on T-shirts, games, and toys. This is called merchandising, and it makes lots of money for the film producers.

Well, that's how *Harald and the Giant Knight* would be made into an animated cartoon. It would take about six months to finish this show. The animators would have to make between 14 000 and 25 000 drawings. It seems like a lot of work for just one half hour of cartoon fun, doesn't it? But wouldn't it be worth it if, one Saturday morning, you woke up to find Harald had come to life on your TV screen?!

FOLLOW UP

Creating an animated film is not simple! That's why the author broke down the process into smaller steps. "Step-by-step" is a useful way to explain how to do something.

Personal Response Do you think *Harald and the Giant Knight* would make a good animated film? Why or why not?

Understanding the Article

From Book to Animation

- Many people with different talents work for an animation company. How would each of these people help to turn *Harald and the Giant Knight* into an animated film?
  - the scriptwriter
  - the storyboard artist
  - the sound technician
  - the background artist
  - the animators
  - the ink and paint artists
  - the editor
- Which of these jobs would you most like to do?

YOUR TURN TO WRITE

Step-by-Step Instructions

Think of something that you know how to do well, like:

a skateboarding trick
playing the guitar
choosing a good book

Then write a set of step-by-step instructions. Explain how to do the activity to someone who has never done it.

Step 1: The first thing you do is...

Step 2: The next thing you do is...

Step 3: When that's done, the next thing is...

Step 4: One of the most important things is...

Use as many steps as you need to describe how the activity is done.

Design a Poster

Work in groups of four or five students. Your task is to create a big poster for the new animated show, *Harald and the Giant Knight*. Decide which scene from the story you want to illustrate. Then divide up these jobs:

- background artist
- ink and paint artists
- writers

1. Paint the background onto a large piece of Bristol board.
2. Draw and paint the characters. Cut out the drawings and paste them onto the background.
3. Add the words last using a marker pen. Write a poster title, information about where and when the show is playing, and quotes from reviews.
4. Display your poster in the classroom.

Imagine!

You're the sound technician for *Harald and the Giant Knight*. You've been asked to record sound effects for galloping horses, clashing swords, clanging pots, moaning sounds, and the giant's deep creaky voice. How will you do it?

BEFORE READING

We wanted to know if an animator would change anything about *Harald and the Giant Knight* before making it into a film. So Susan Hughes talked to Gary Pearson to find out.

Talking with an Animator

Article by
Susan Hughes

Gary Pearson is an animator. He's a funny, talented guy who draws cartoons and makes animated films. He works for the CBC (Canadian Broadcasting Corporation). He has done animation for children's shows such as *Sesame Park* and *Mr. Dressup,* as well as *Hockey Night in Canada* and the Olympic Games. He talked to Susan about how he became an animator and how he would animate a story you know well— *Harald and the Giant Knight.*

How I Became an Animator

"Sitting at a table and drawing cartoon characters—that's a pretty good job! It's fun to make my characters move and give them personalities. It's fun to make them seem real when they are really just drawings on a piece of paper.

"I've been interested in animated films since I was a child. I watched a lot of cartoons on television. I liked to draw the characters. I would draw, draw, draw all the time.

"When I was about 14, I started making 'flip' books. I would draw characters in the margins of the pages. As I flipped the pages with my thumb, the characters would walk and jump and the rockets would take off. That's animation!

"I studied graphic arts and illustration at Sheridan College for three years. I remember making an animated film in a film class. Was it good? Well, let's say that it taught me some things! In fact, that's still true today. Every film I do teaches me something more. I watch my finished film and I discover what I like about it —and what I don't like. That's the way I learn.

"I love it best when I create a film all on my own. I come up with the idea, I do the storyboard, and then I do the drawings and the paintings. That's very satisfying."

How I Would Animate Harald

"Sometimes the idea for an animated film comes from a children's book. Just look at *Harald and the Giant Knight*. I think it would make a good half-hour show for television. But what works on a printed page doesn't always work as a film. There are some changes I would make if I were making this story into an animated film.

"In the story, Harald gets close to a group of knights. When he discovers what the knights are really like, he's disenchanted. This works well as a print story. But in a film, getting to know one particular knight would have more impact on an audience. I would call the one knight, "Sir Knight." Harald would still be fond of all knights, but Sir Knight would be his hero.

"It would be fun to make Sir Knight's character comic—all puffed up with self-importance. Harald doesn't realize this until he gets to know him well. When Harald becomes disenchanted with Sir Knight, he also becomes disenchanted with all the knights.

"Another thing—I would flesh out the character of Harald's father. There is an interesting triangle here. Where does the boy's heart belong? With his father, the hardworking farmer, or with the flashy knight? The film could emphasize the visual contrasts. Sir Knight would look like a hero, although he turns out not to be. The father could look rather plain and have a sense of humour about himself, but end up being the real hero.

"I would use humour all the way through. But I would especially enjoy recreating the scene of Harald and his parents scaring the knights with the giant scarecrow knight. This is the comic pay-off. I would make this a fun, slapstick sequence!"

> 66 **I love it best when I create a film all on my own.** 99

FOLLOW UP

Were you surprised by any of Gary Pearson's ideas for changing the story? Would you change anything else about the story if you were animating it? Explain.

Make Your Own Flip Book

Gary Pearson says he used to make flip books. They are a good way to see how animation works.
Try creating your own animated cartoon. Give it a title.

1. You'll need a small notebook with lots of pages, and a pencil that makes strong, dark lines.

2. Start on the right side of the first page. Draw a simple cartoon character in the act of doing something — like running, diving, or kicking a ball. Press hard with your pencil.

3. On the next page, trace over the marks your pencil made, but change your drawing slightly. For example, draw the kicking foot and ball a little higher. Go on doing this on each page to the end of the notebook.

4. Now flip through the pages with your thumb — and watch your character move!

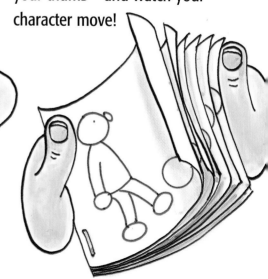

Secrets of an Animator

- How did Gary Pearson show his interest in animation when he was young?
- How did he turn his early interest into a career?
- Why do you think Gary Pearson would create a character called "Sir Knight"?
- Do you agree with Gary that the animated film of Harald should be really funny? Why or why not?

Imagine!

You're the scriptwriter working on *Harald and the Giant Knight.* The film producer comes to you and says, "We need a girl in this story!" How would you solve this problem?

MORE GOOD READING

❦ The White Stone in the Castle Wall
by Sheldon Oberman

Casa Loma is a magnificent castle in the middle of Toronto. In the wall there is one white stone. How did it get there? This imaginative book tells the story of a poor boy who brought the stone up the hill—and met the builder of the castle. (a picture book)

A Samurai Castle
by Fiona MacDonald

Castles in Japan look quite different from European castles. But they also served as homes to knights, called samurai. This beautifully illustrated book shows how the castles were built, how the samurai were trained, and how their families lived. (an information book)

The Adventures of King Arthur Retold
by Angela Wilkes

If you enjoyed reading *The Sword in the Stone,* you might want to find out about King Arthur's other great adventures. With colourful pictures Angela Wilkes retells Arthur's encounter with the lady of the lake, his gathering of the loyal Knights of the Round Table, and his love for his Queen Guinevere. (legends)

Animation
by Janine Amos

Like to know more about making animated films? This book uses colourful cartoon drawings and easy-to-follow text to take you through the whole process. It has fun activities, too! (an information book)

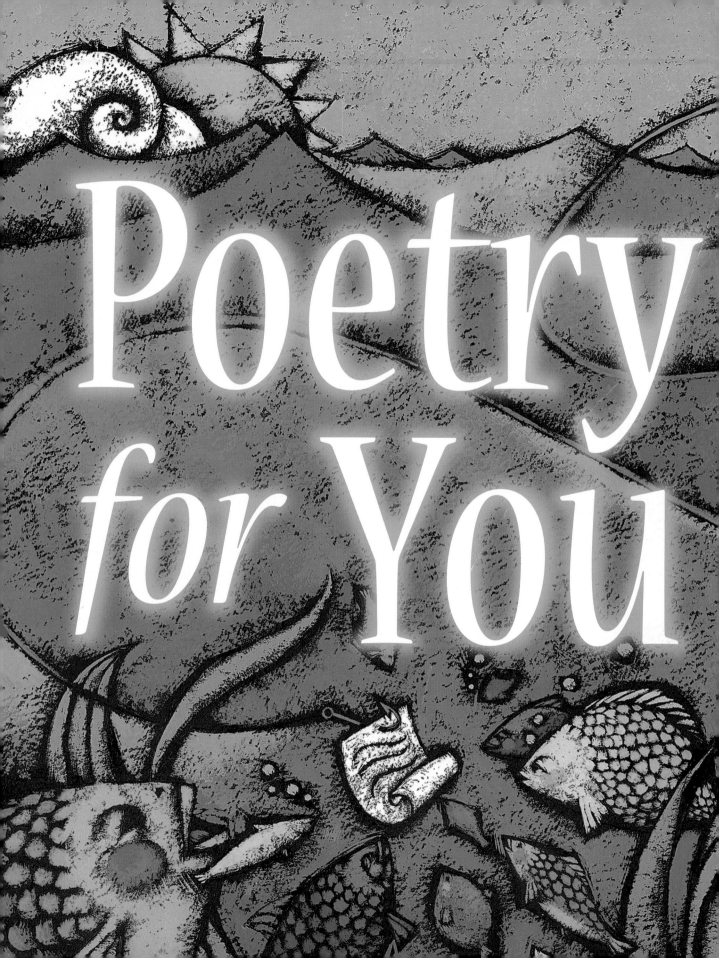

Poetry for You

Poets Go Wishing

Poem by Lilian Moore

**Poets go fishing
with buckets
of words,
fishing
and wishing.**

**Using a line
that's loose or
tight
(Maybe this time
a rhyme is
right.)**

**Unreeling
unreeling
the words till they
match
the feeling the poet is
trying to
catch.**

BEAST *feast*

Poems by Douglas Florian   Pictures by Chum McLeod

The Boa

Just when you think you know the boa,

There's moa and moa and moa and moa.

The Anteater

The
anteater's
long
and
tacky
tongue
is
snaking
from
its
snout.

The Firefly

On August nights
The firefly lights
Blink
ON and OFF
Amongst the trees
But have no need
For batteries.

A thousand termites riding in,
But no one riding out.

3 Haiku

Pictures by Jackie Besteman

Conversation

An umbrella
And a raincoat
Are walking and talking together

by Buson

Empty circus tent

Empty circus tent:
from the high wire—a spider
swings on its thread

by George Swede

That duck, bobbing up

That duck, bobbing up
from the green deeps of a pond,
has seen something strange.

by Joso

POET'S CRAFT

Beast Feast

1. Looks Like Fun — Shapes

- Why did Douglas Florian shape his poems the way he did?

- Which shape do you think works the best?

2. Sounds Like Fun — Rhyme

Here is an example of one of Douglas Florian's rhymes:

> On August *nights*
> The firefly *lights*...

- Find the other pairs of rhyming words in Florian's three poems.

- Which word has an invented spelling? Why do you think the poet spelled it this way?

A "Beast Feast" Poem

Try writing a poem of your own to add to the "Beast Feast." Have fun giving it a shape (like an elephant's trunk!). Use rhyme too, if you like.

Which of the *Beast Feast* poems is your favourite? To read more, look for Douglas Florian's poem-and-picture book, *Beast Feast!*

A Gift from Japan — the Haiku

Haiku poems have been written in Japan for centuries. A haiku is a short poem that freezes a moment in time.

In Japanese, haiku have three short lines and seventeen syllables. The first line has five syllables, the second seven, and the third five.

When haiku are written in English, the number of lines and syllables often changes. But every haiku should be like a snapshot with a little surprise.

- Count the syllables in *Empty circus tent, Conversation,* and *That duck, bobbing up.*

  Which one has seventeen syllables?

- What are the "little surprises" in these three haiku?

the visitor

poem by **sean o huigan**   *picture by* **don gauthier**

one night
i woke up
when the
rest were
asleep
and felt
something
crawly
that started
to creep
up my arm
'neath the
covers
i brushed
it away
but it
didn't go
it wanted
to stay

it creepy
crawled
slowly
with long
hairy
steps
it tickled
and
whispered
and got to
my neck
it sssssssed
and it husssssshhhhhed
and it sssssshhhhhhhhhed
and it haaaaaaaahhhhed
it creeped 'cross
my face
and it felt
very odd
it crawled
'round my shoulders
and crept down
my back
then spidered
away
and hid
in the
black

The Purple Cow

Poem by **Gelett Burgess**
Picture by **Susan Ashukian**

I never saw a Purple Cow,
I never hope to see one;
But I can tell you, anyhow,
I'd rather see than be one.

Purple Cow

Poem by **Lois Simmie**

The day I saw a purple cow
While riding on my bike,
I hopped right off and asked that cow
What being one was like.

She gave me such a gloomy look
And cried a purple tear;
Her droopy tail swished slow and sad
Behind her purple rear.

"It's very rude," she softly mooed,
"That no one wants to see you;
And when they do they tell you that
They'd rather see than be you."

"It makes me mad and *mooo*dy,
It makes me sad and bloo;
I *mooo*n around and chew my cud,
That's all I ever doo."

I hopped my bike and rode away
And never went back to see her,
But I can tell you anyhow,
I'd rather see than be her.

Read It Aloud

Get together with a group of two or three friends and plan a dramatic reading of *the visitor*. Make your reading as creepy as possible. Here are some hints:

- Start reading softly and build up the volume to the scariest line.
- Decide who will say which lines, alone or together.
- Give a little extra emphasis to the repetitions of the word "it."
- Think about possible movements you could make.

- When you perform the poem, turn down the lights.

POET'S CRAFT

Find the Metre!

The Purple Cow poems have a regular beat (or metre). Try reading the first verse of Lois Simmie's poem aloud. Clap on the strong beats! Here's how to show the beats (or metre) in poetry. This mark [ˇ] shows the light beats. This mark [/] shows the strong beats.

> The dˇay I/ sˇaw a/ pˇurple/ cˇow While/ rˇiding/ on mˇy/ bike,

This kind of metre is called *iambic* — the first syllable has a light beat, the second a strong beat, and so on. Poems can have many different metres.

"Da-dum, da-dum, da-dum, da-dum!"

- Copy the second verse of Lois Simmie's *Purple Cow* into your notebook. Mark the light and strong beats.
- Now try the same thing with *The Purple Cow* by Gelett Burgess. Which lines have one extra light beat?
- Which lines of Lois Simmie's *Purple Cow* have the same extra beat?

TIP To find the beats in a poem, it's always better to read it aloud.

Responding Activities **151**

 Grass Song

Poem by **Ellen Bryan Obed**   Picture by **Shawn Steffler**

Witchgrass, stitchgrass, in-the-roadside-ditch grass;
Junegrass, strewn grass, waving-on-the-dune grass;
   Everywhere I pass, grass. Everywhere I see

Bluegrass, new grass, wet-with-morning-dew grass;
Sniff grass, stiff grass, growing-on-the-cliff grass;
   Everywhere I pass, grass. Everywhere I see

Fox-tail, squirrel-tail, standing-brown-and-stale grass;
Barley, timothy, tickles-on-the-knee grass;
   Everywhere I pass, grass. Everywhere I see

Clump grass, stump grass, even-in-the-dump grass;
Moose grass, goose grass, anyone can use grass;
Sweet grass, peat grass — we can even EAT grass!
   Everywhere I pass, grass — and grasses pass me!

Let's Sing of Strawberries

Poem by Ellen Bryan Obed   Picture by Shawn Steffler

Let's sing of strawberries
    for shortcake and pie
when there's a fragrant breeze
    and a ripening sky.

Let's walk to the patch
    that hides in the hay
with baskets and dippers
    for a strawberry day.

We'll bend in the grasses
    until the evening comes;
then with strawberry faces
    and strawberry thumbs,

We'll go home with strawberries
    for shortcake and pie
as the strawberry sun
    stains a strawberry sky.

Portrait of a Poet

Ellen Bryan Obed began writing poetry at the age of eleven. Her favourite place to write was sitting under an apple tree on her family's farm. In high school, her friends helped her to publish her first book.

Ellen has lived many years in the North, in Labrador. Ideas for poems come while she's hiking, canoeing, or just being outdoors. She says the lines of her poems over and over again, out loud. When she's ready to write, she sits at her desk with a pencil.

Besides *Wind in My Pocket* (poetry), Ellen's published books are *Little Snowshoe* and *Borrowed Black: A Labrador Fantasy*.

POET'S CRAFT

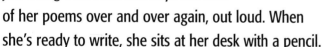

Metaphor

"My favourite kind of writing is poetry," says Ellen. "I can say something intensely and deeply and clearly in poetry. In the poem *Let's Sing of Strawberries*, I call the sunset a strawberry staining the sky. In another of my poems, *The Robin Sang*, I call the sunset a 'robin's breast'."

When Ellen compares the sunset to strawberry juice staining the sky, or to the red of a robin's breast, she is using **metaphor**.

- Brainstorm with a small group of students. Think of metaphors you could use to complete this sentence: "A sunset is..."

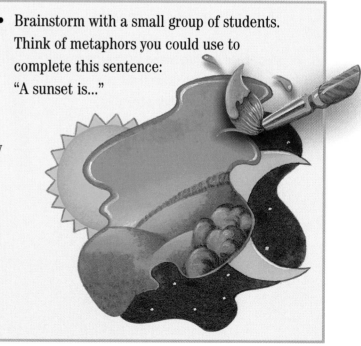

THE Snowflake

Poem by *Walter de la Mare*
Picture by *Daphne McCormick*

Before I melt,
Come, look at me!
This lovely icy filigree!
Of a great forest
In one night
I make a wilderness
Of white:
By skyey cold
Of crystals made,
All softly, on
Your finger laid,
I pause, that you
My beauty see:
Breathe, and I vanish
Instantly.

Cold Spell

Poem by Monica Kulling
Picture by Heather Holbrook

All day long
Ravens
Carve their
Tapered silken wings
Into the
Cold winter sky.

Hurricane

Poem by Dionne Brand

Shut the windows
Bolt the doors
Big rain coming
Climbing up the mountain.

Neighbours whisper
Dark clouds gather
Big rain coming
Climbing up the mountain.

Gather in the clothes lines
Pull down the blinds
Big wind rising
Coming up the mountain.

Branches falling
Raindrops flying
Tree tops swaying
People running
Big wind blowing
Hurricane! on the mountain.

Choral Reading

How would you feel if a hurricane was coming? If you lived on a Caribbean island, you would get plenty of chances to find out. Dionne Brand gives us a vivid picture of people getting ready to face a big storm.

Get together with a small group. How would you create a dramatic presentation of *Hurricane*?

- Think about the wild action in the poem — the rain, the wind, and the people.

- Listen to the breathless feeling in the poem's short lines.

- Notice the refrain, "Climbing up the mountain," and how Dionne repeats it and changes it.

Putting on a Mask— The Snowflake

What would it be like to be someone — or something – other than yourself? That's what Walter de la Mare has imagined. He has put on a snowflake mask to write his poem.

- What are some of the thoughts and feelings he has as a snowflake?

- How does he show us snowflakes in a new way?

- What part of the weather would you like to pretend to be? A whirlwind, a tornado, a drop of rain, or something else? Write a poem about what you're doing and how you're feeling. Let your imagination go!

TIP Be sure to use the pronouns "I" and "me" in your poem.

An Acrostic Poem

Monica Kulling's poem has a hidden message. Read it from top to bottom as well as from left to right! To write her poem, Monica began with the word "ARCTIC," then filled in the lines later. This is a fun way to create a poem. Try it yourself using a weather word, or your own name.

I Left My Head

Poem by Lilian Moore

Pictures by Pierre-Paul Pariseau

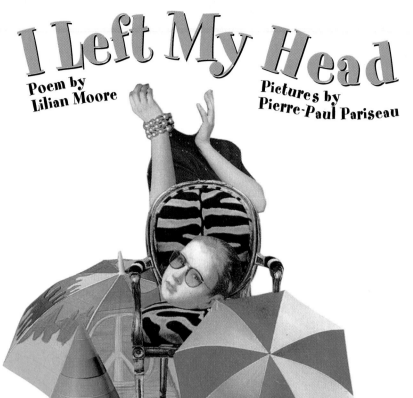

I left my head
somewhere
today.
Put it down for
just
a minute.
Under the
table?
On a chair?
Wish I were
able
to say
where.
Everything I need
is
in it!

Fame Was a Claim of Uncle Ed's

Poem by Ogden Nash

Fame was a claim of Uncle Ed's,
Simply because he had three heads,
Which, if he'd only had a third of,
I think he would never have been
heard of.

Create a Poetry Scrapbook

You know that poetry can be funny, sad, mysterious, and exciting. Why not make a collection of your favourite poems? You could choose a theme, like Nonsense or Seasons or Animals or People. Do a big library search. Ask the grown-ups at home to contribute some poems, too. Paste one poem on each page of your scrapbook. Then illustrate the poems with drawings or photographs.

A Cinquain

Here is a new form of poem you might like to try—a "cinquain." It has five lines. This example is by a student called Stanley. On the right, the dashes show the number of syllables he used (2, 4, 6, 8, 2).

The Storm
Thunder!   — —
Lightning flashing!   — — — —
Black moonless, starless sky;   — — — — — —
Thunder rolling like a bass drum.   — — — — — — — —
The storm.   — —

Try writing your own cinquain. The only "rule" is to stick to the number of syllables shown in each line. Choose a subject, then describe it in a fresh way!

MORE GOOD READING

☀ Aska's Sea Creatures by Warabé Aska and David Day
This book is a journey into an exotic underwater world. You'll find yourself swimming alongside the huge but graceful sea turtle, the tiny shining starfish, the terrible great white shark, and many other sea creatures.

The Dragons Are Singing Tonight by Jack Prelutsky
After reading these incredible poems, and falling under the spell of the extraordinary pictures, you will have to believe in dragons!

☀ Till All the Stars Have Fallen: Canadian Poems for Children Edited by David Booth
This anthology is the perfect place to find a poem about the place where you live, or the seasons you experience, or the kinds of people you know. Happy or sad, funny or serious, there are poems for everyone here.

Walking the Bridge of Your Nose by Michael Rosen
A feast of poems and rhymes that play with language. You'll love the mouth-mangling tongue-twisters and perplexing word puzzles. Welcome to the world of nonsense!

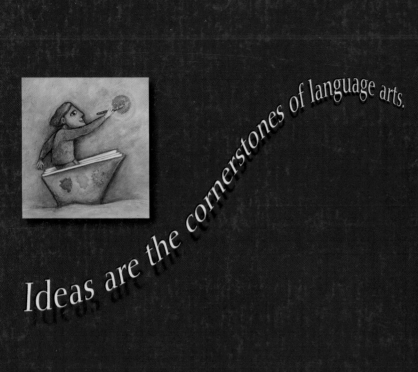

Ideas are the cornerstones of language arts.

gage

Cornerstones

3a   3b

4a   **4b**

5a   5b

6a   6b

Book
CBE0-0063-9744

DO NOT REMOVE

ISBN 0-7715-1201-5

90000

9 780771 512018

T2-AGR-725